Management 2000

The American Foundation for Management Research Manager Learning Center, Hamilton, New York

Management 2000

Dedication of the
AFMR Manager Learning Center and
Donald W. Mitchell Memorial Library
Hamilton, New York
August 1967

THE AMERICAN FOUNDATION FOR MANAGEMENT RESEARCH
Founded by the American Management Association

Foreword

Mankind owes much of its progress to those leaders who have looked to the future, who have sought and recognized a better way and had the courage to depart from the established order when necessary. A characteristic of the successful American manager in every phase of our economy is his ability and willingness to change; to innovate, improve, modify, or adapt his management philosophy, practices, and skills to new and different needs or conditions, to new technology, to new facts or knowledge; in short, to manage his organization in such a manner that the future can become reality.

The time span between the conception and the implementation of ideas for new and better ways continues to shrink. Each day additional—and vital—information becomes available. If the present rate of shrinkage continues to the year 2000, will management—that is, the responsible decision makers in business, education, labor, government, and other phases of the world's activity—be able to understand the implications of the new discoveries and make proper use of the new knowledge that will have accumulated? Will yesterday's technological gap be replaced tomorrow by a management gap? What skills and educational preparation will our managers in the year 2000 need?

A sharing of management experience and knowledge will be as important to future managers as it is to today's. Just as certainly as the international activities of our U.S. companies will continue to result in improved managerial techniques both here and abroad, so too will intranational cross-fertilization of ideas and practices among these same American companies help insure that our managers have the skills and preparation necessary to function successfully in the

21st century. Forums like the one on "Management 2000" reported in this book, the research and manager learning activities of The American Foundation for Management Research, the many management education programs of the American Management Association and other organizations—all will help keep U.S. managers in the forefront of their profession.

The American Foundation for Management Research, a nonprofit organization, was founded by AMA in 1960. The Foundation has administrative and research offices in New York City and a Manager Learning Center in Hamilton, New York. A permanent building for the Center, whose unique approach to working with an organization's executive team makes it possible, in a short period of time, to introduce modern concepts and techniques directly into management practices at the highest levels of that organization, was dedicated on August 22, 1967. On that occasion, leaders in diverse sectors of our society presented their views on "Management 2000." Their stimulating, imaginative, thought-provoking ideas are contained in this volume, and their significant contribution to management of the future is gratefully acknowledged.

LAWRENCE A. APPLEY
President,
American Management Association
The American Foundation for Management Research

ARTHUR W. ANGRIST
Vice President and Managing Director,
The American Foundation for Management Research

Contents

Program 11

    Monday 15
    11:00 A.M. *to 12:00* NOON 17

Greetings *by Don G. Mitchell* 17
Opening Remarks *by Dr. Arthur W. Angrist* 18
Remarks on Behalf of AFMR Advisory Council *by Dr. Lillian M. Gilbreth* 21
Address: "The AFMR Manager Learning Center: Its Purposes, Philosophy, and Operations" *by Merritt L. Kastens* 25

    1:00 to 2:00 P.M. 33

Introduction *by Dr. Arthur W. Angrist* 33
Address: "The Impact of Higher Education upon the Management Environment in the Year 2000" *by Dr. Vincent M. Barnett, Jr.* 34

    2:15 to 4:30 P.M. 47

Opening Remarks *by Dr. Arthur W. Angrist* 47
Panel: "The State of Information Retrieval and Data Processing in the Year 2000 and Its Implications for Management" 48
    Introduction *by Henry M. Boettinger* 48
    Presentation *by Dr. C. W. Churchman* 50
    Presentation *by William T. Knox* 54
    Presentation *by Norman J. Ream* 59
    Discussion 82

    7:30 to 9:30 P.M. 98

Opening Remarks *by Dr. Arthur W. Angrist* 98
Panel: "Implications of the Behavioral Sciences on Management Practices in the Year 2000" 99

7

Introduction *by Dr. S. C. Hollister* 99
Presentation *by Dr. Bernard M. Bass* 101
Presentation *by Dr. Edwin R. Henry* 107
Presentation *by Dr. Forrest H. Kirkpatrick* 113
Discussion 121

Tuesday 135
8:30 to 10:15 A.M. 137

Introduction *by Don G. Mitchell* 137
Opening Remarks *by Lee S. Bickmore* 138
Address: "Management in Retrospect" *by Dr. Clarence C. Walton* 139
Address: "Government and the Manager in the Year 2000" *by Elmer B. Staats* 151

10:30 A.M. *to 12:00* NOON 167

Opening Remarks *by Lee S. Bickmore* 167
Address: "Management Leadership in the Year 2000" *by Frank J. Nunlist* 168
Address: "Educational Preparation for the Manager in 2000" *by Dr. Herbert E. Longenecker* 177

12:00 NOON *to 1:00* P.M. 193

Opening Remarks *by Don G. Mitchell* 193
Invocation *by Reverend Vernon H. Ross* 193
Explanation of the Time Capsule *by Merritt L. Kastens* 195
Dedication Address *by Lawrence A. Appley* 199
Benediction *by Reverend Matthew J. Doran* 207

Illustrations

Frontispiece, The American Foundation for Management Research Manager Learning Center, Hamilton, New York

The following photographs are grouped in a separate section between pages 112 and 113

Lawrence A. Appley, President of AMA and AFMR, standing beside the oil painting of the late Donald W. Mitchell

Dr. Arthur W. Angrist, Vice President and Managing Director of AFMR

Donald G. Mitchell, Chairman, Board of Directors and Executive Committee, AMA

Guests in the Donald W. Mitchell Memorial Library

Mr. Appley, on the Flag Terrace, dedicating the Manager Learning Center

Dr. Lillian M. Gilbreth, life member of AMA and charter member of AFMR

Merritt L. Kastens, Director of the AFMR Manager Learning Center

The Chandelier Room of the AFMR Manager Learning Center

The Time Capsule, containing records of current management practices, to be opened August 22, 2000

9

Program

General Chairman: Don G. Mitchell

Chairman of the Board of General Time Corporation

and of the American Management Association

SUNDAY, AUGUST 20

2:00-5:00 P.M.

Open House at the Center

MONDAY, AUGUST 21

11:00-11:30 A.M.—Donald W. Mitchell Memorial Library

Opening Remarks—Dr. Arthur W. Angrist,
AFMR Vice President and Managing Director

Remarks on Behalf of AFMR Advisory Council
Dr. Lillian M. Gilbreth, Charter Member

11:30 A.M.-12:00 NOON

"The AFMR Manager Learning Center: Its Purposes, Philosophy, and Operations"
Merritt L. Kastens, Director, AFMR Manager Learning Center

12:15-1:00 P.M.—Lower Lounge

Luncheon

1:00-1:15 P.M.—Library

Introduction of Session Chairman Dr. Arthur W. Angrist

1:15-2:00 P.M.

"The Impact of Higher Education upon the Management Environment in the Year 2000"
Dr. Vincent M. Barnett, Jr., President, Colgate University

2:15-4:30 P.M.—Substance Center 5

Panel: "The State of Information Retrieval and Data Processing in the Year 2000 and Its Implications for Management"

Panel Chairman: Henry M. Boettinger, Assistant Comptroller, American Telephone and Telegraph Company

Panel Members:

Dr. C. W. Churchman, Associate Director, Space Sciences Laboratory and Professor of Business Administration, University of California (Berkeley)

William T. Knox, Vice President, Information Services, McGraw-Hill Company

Norman J. Ream, Special Assistant to the Secretary of the Navy

5:00-6:00 P.M.—Chandelier Room
Refreshments

6:00-7:00 P.M.—Lower Lounge
Dinner

7:30-9:30 P.M.—Substance Center 5

Panel: "Implications of the Behavioral Sciences on Management Practices in the Year 2000"

Panel Chairman: Dr. S. C. Hollister, Dean Emeritus, College of Engineering, Cornell University

Panel Members:

Dr. Bernard M. Bass, Director, Management Research Center, Graduate School of Business, University of Pittsburgh

Dr. Edwin R. Henry, Professor, College of Business Administration, University of Rochester

Dr. Forrest H. Kirkpatrick, Vice President and Secretary, Wheeling Steel Corporation

TUESDAY, AUGUST 22

8:30-8:45 A.M.—Substance Center 5

Introduction of Chairman Lee S. Bickmore, President, National Biscuit Company

8:45-9:30 A.M.

"Management in Retrospect"

Dr. Clarence C. Walton, Dean of the School of General Studies, Columbia University

9:30-10:15 A.M.

"Government and the Manager in the Year 2000"

Elmer B. Staats, Comptroller General of the United States

10:15-10:30 A.M.—Lower Lounge

Refreshments

10:30-11:15 A.M.

"Management Leadership in the Year 2000"

Frank J. Nunlist, Chairman of the Board and Chief Executive Officer, Worthington Corporation

11:15 A.M.-12:00 NOON

"Educational Preparation for the Manager in 2000"

Dr. Herbert E. Longenecker, President, Tulane University

12:00-1:00 P.M.—Dedication Ceremony, Flag Terrace

Invocation: Reverend Vernon H. Ross, First Baptist Church, Hamilton

Time Capsule: Merritt L. Kastens

Introduction of Dedication Speaker by Don G. Mitchell

Dedication Address: Lawrence A. Appley, President, American Management Association and The American Foundation for Management Research

Benediction: Reverend Matthew J. Doran, St. Mary's Catholic Church, Hamilton

MONDAY

August 21

Greetings

DON G. MITCHELL
Chairman of the Board, General Time Corporation, and
Chairman of the Board, American Management Association

I am most pleased to be here to help signalize the opening of this Manager Learning Center and the Donald W. Mitchell Memorial Library by The American Foundation for Management Research.

As its name implies, the Center is devoted to manager learning. As most of you know, I have devoted a great portion of my life to the pursuit of manager learning and to assisting others in that effort. I believe that a better present and a better future for all of us are largely dependent upon professional management. The most efficient utilization of the world's resources by government, education, business, industry, and agriculture is essential to a better life for everyone everywhere. Professional management is the key to the best use of our physical and human resources. I know that Larry Appley shares this opinion, and I am confident that our eminent speakers and panelists share it too.

The existence of this building, the very existence of The American Foundation for Management Research, is the strongest testimony that the American Management Association is actively planning for the future of professional management. AMA founded The American Foundation for Management Research in 1960 as part of its effort, not only to develop new management knowledge, but to aid in the effective utilization of that knowledge. This Manager Learning Center is a major contribution by AMA and its related organizations to the development of professional management. But this is only the most recent, and perhaps the most spectacular, of a long series of achievements by AMA. I am confident that there will be many more.

Now I would like to introduce to you Dr. Arthur Angrist, vice president and managing director of The American Foundation for Management Research. Dr. Angrist will outline the purposes of The American Foundation for Management Research, of which this Center is so significant a part.

Dr. Angrist has had distinguished careers in both education and industry. He received his B.A. and M.A. from the University of Michigan and his Ph.D. in industrial psychology and communications from Ohio State. He has been a member of the faculty of two universities and has held a number of management positions with the Ford Motor Company.

Opening Remarks

DR. ARTHUR W. ANGRIST
AFMR Vice President and Managing Director

It is a pleasure and a privilege for me to welcome you here this morning on behalf of The American Foundation for Management Research and the American Management Association.

As Mr. Mitchell has mentioned, the Foundation was established in 1960 by the American Management Association. It is a not-for-profit institution with educational and scientific purposes in the field of management.

So that the nature of the Foundation's activities may be better understood, and the scope of its potential influence and application more readily appreciated, let me state briefly what we mean by the term "management." Consistent with the definition of the term as used by the American Management Association, we consider management a part of the coordination of human effort and material resources to create and increase social values. In addition, management is a function that is found in all organizations, in all segments of our society, in profit-making organizations as well as in nonprofit institutions, such as government, universities, labor unions, and so forth. Furthermore, the professional approach to management includes the systematic and orderly collection, classification, and analysis of the growing body of management knowledge and experience. The educational and scientific purposes of the Foundation are reflected in its two major activities, manager learning research and its Manager Learning Center.

No organization can successfully fulfill its goals without management. All businesses require management, but no more so than hospitals, universities, military organizations, departments of government, philanthropic foundations, or any other institution.

Now, one of the characteristics of successful management is the willingness and ability to change—to innovate, improve, modify, or adapt to meet new or different needs, conditions, or circumstances, to adapt to new technology and to new facts or knowledge. To learn is to change. Yet, given the crucial importance of the manager in all aspects of our society, relatively little research has been done into the learning process as it occurs in the actual management environment. Empirical research into learning under these conditions has been sparse.

More information about manager learning could have considerable social value, since we are speaking of the men and women who manage so many aspects of our affairs. What has been discovered about the learning process and behavior patterns from studies of high school students and college students is certainly valuable information. But also of considerable value is the corresponding information relating to our nation's managers. AFMR's manager learning research is intended to contribute to the fund of knowledge about manager learning.

From a refinement and development of some of the findings of studies conducted by AFMR shortly after it was founded evolved the concepts, processes, and techniques that we have today in this Manager Learning Center. All that exists here is designed to assist management in its efforts to manage more effectively. Among the manager's most urgent responsibilities is that of preparing himself and his enterprise for the future. And, just as certainly as managing today is more complex than it was yesterday, so will it be increasingly complex tomorrow.

Because the Manager Learning Center is designed to help today's managers cope with the future, the theme for the dedication of this Center is especially appropriate. Here, for two days, we will be examining with distinguished leaders in business, government, and education the subject of *Management 2000.*

What will a manager at the start of the new century be like? What sort of education will he require? How will the technology of the time serve him? There could be no more fitting place than this, no more fitting time than now—since the graduates of today will be the managers in the next century—to examine such truly stimulating, challenging, and important questions.

MR. MITCHELL: As you can see, Dr. Angrist and his staff are in the forefront of the effort to develop our future knowledge about management. Now I would like to introduce you to a lady who has been leading the way to greater knowledge in management for a long time.

On second thought, I think the word "introduce" is wrong. There are not many of you who do not already know her. I would rather say that I am honored to present you to Dr. Lillian M. Gilbreth.

Dr. Gilbreth is a most distinguished figure in the world of professional management. With her husband, Frank Bunker Gilbreth, she was a pioneer in the field, and at the age of 89 she is still more active than most of us in the work of many management organizations.

The list of meetings she attended and her platform appearances all over the United States and Europe and the Far East for the year 1966 alone would require a full page of single-spaced typing. She is the author of at least eight books and innumerable articles on professional management, methods of aiding the handicapped, and the application of psychology and physiology in work and home situations.

In addition to her achievements in the world of education, engineering, and management, Dr. Gilbreth raised a family of 12 and, at last count, is the grandmother of 29. During this public and personal career she found time to write several children's books.

Now, it doesn't say so here, Dr. Gilbreth, but . . .

DR. GILBRETH: My children wrote them.

MR. MITCHELL: Your children wrote the books. Yes, we all know one that your son Frank and one of your daughters wrote. But you did this in Montclair, and Montclair is where I lived the first 30 years of my life. I was a classmate of one of your daughters all through Montclair High School.]

Dr. Gilbreth, who obtained her Ph.D. at Brown University in 1915, has been awarded a dozen honorary degrees and innumerable medals. In late 1966 she was presented with the Hoover Medal for her "contributions to motion study and to recognition of the principle that management engineering and human relations are intertwined." She is a recipient of the Henry Lawrence Gantt Medal, a life member of the American Management Association, and a charter member of the Advisory Council of The American Foundation for Management Research.

Remarks on Behalf of AFMR Advisory Council

DR. LILLIAN M. GILBRETH
AFMR Charter Member

It has been a great pleasure to be a member of AMA for so long, and also to have a part in the work of this committee—the AFMR Advisory Council—which concerns itself with research. We of this committee need, if we're to do a really good job, an interest on your part in contributing what you've done, what you're thinking about, exactly what your plans are. It would be very stimulating; in fact, I think the returns we make to you are bound to be very largely dependent upon the questions you ask and the answers you give. There's much work to be done in this field—by everybody.

When we look at this matter of management, it's obvious that we need a better definition than many which are used. I have occasion to look in dictionaries very often, not only for my own needs but for my students'. And students—especially the ones who come from other countries—need to know more about our actual experience with words and what they signify.

So let's take the word "management" and look it up in the dictionary. There are one or two rather good definitions which give us some idea of what it is. But it's when we come down to the examples showing the use of the word that we see what confusion exists. This is true of many, many words—not only in the minds of our own people but, above all, in the minds of people abroad, even those with the best education. For instance, the dictionary may say that management has to do with the reactions of human beings. Very good. Then, when we come to the illustration, it seems that the manager may be "a very devious person . . . often a woman."

I could endure the first part of this definition; the second part really is very distressing! And the examples which are given convey a very poor idea of what we mean by management in the sense of accepting responsibility for an organization or other sphere of human activity.

However, let's turn from this light-hearted talking about management to a consideration of what it *really* is—the significance and use of the term. So far as the word in industry is concerned, I think its usage was determined by some of the early groups in the field.

The engineering group, for example, defines management as "the utilization of the resources of nature and human nature for the benefit of mankind." This is a highly useful and impressive statement of exactly what we're hoping to do. We state this very often when we start our books, our lectures, our conferences, or our talks; but especially when out of the country we sometimes *omit* to state it, and it's very necessary that we do state that we're trying to use these resources.

Why do we use these resources of nature and of human nature? Not to make more money. Not to get to more places. Not even to get a certain amount of fame, but to use these *for the benefit of mankind.* Now, "mankind" does not mean only the U.S.A., and it does not mean the "civilized world," so to speak. It means just what it says—all mankind. And, as we go on in this work, we're going to realize this more and more. Also, we're going to have to start very young—with the children. I don't know whether any of you have come across a book which is just about ready to be published, but I happen to have read the galley proofs. It tells what is happening to the education of children, how education starts just as soon as the child is born. This is very interesting to me—the idea of the parents not only wanting the child but wanting to educate him from the start. There should be much of this not only in this country but in other countries.

I remember very well the time when the idea of trying to teach a child anything just as soon as he was born would frighten the parents and everybody else. They would think to themselves that they would just strain the child's brain or do something else terrible to him.

I remember how Frank, my husband, thought that this sort of early start was a perfectly doable thing, a wonderful thing. When our first little daughter was just a day old, he said to me, "Do you mind if I put her in the tub to see if she can swim or not?" Well, I did mind, though I didn't say anything about it because I thought, "Oh, she has to get acquainted with her father." But my mother-in-law, rest her soul, and a sister who lived with us protested very vigorously. I don't think I could have handled the situation, but as usual Frank handled it—and them—very nicely.

He took the nurse and went to the bathroom, and they set up the tub and put the child in. I prayed that everything would go peacefully. In a moment they came out, very much disappointed, and Frank said, "Well, she *can't* swim." He was really chagrined about it. I said, "Give her time." But Frank retorted, "I don't want to give her time. I've given *you* a lot of time." And I tell you confidentially that I really don't swim at all.

So this is the sort of experience we're going to talk about and think about—the individual, his age, his needs. As we well know, these are the terms in which we are looking at management today, and I hope that the studies sponsored by the Foundation will go on

and on and do more and more in this area of human needs and behavior.

We know, too, that there are at least five areas in management
which concern every one of us. The first is managing oneself. Very
few people think about this at all; almost none put it at the beginning of the list. Yet I have found that some of the most brilliant,
most really effective people in the management field cannot manage
themselves. The thing which makes them successful managers—ability to drive others and get things done—is something which from
their own point of view seems to develop naturally out of the need to
get the job done and, therefore, to be quite justifiable. I'm talking
about temper tantrums. Now, temper tantrums may hurt nobody
but the people who have them. But a temper tantrum in industry, a
temper tantrum in one's human relations, is a mistake that the manager has to live down. It's not a tool that he ought to resort to either
instinctively or deliberately.

Then we have management in the family. One of our great problems, of course, is to get people who as managers contribute fully to
the organization which employs them but also save much time for
the family. I'm not going into that problem, but we all know it is a
real one. In contrast, some people give almost too much to the family
and don't have time or energy for the job. At any rate we all have
these two management responsibilities: to manage ourselves and to
manage our family life. And, in addition, we have the management
of our affairs as citizens, the management of community activities as
volunteers, and of course the job of the manager in business, industry, government, research, or whatever.

These five areas of management are important—and they're important in every country in the world. One of the obligations I think
we are going to have increasingly, and already are beginning to feel,
is the obligation to help other nations. We are realizing more and
more that we must share the knowledge we have gained over years of
experience; that, if we don't share it, it isn't worth much. But, on the
other hand, we must give other people a chance to share their knowledge with us too. That's why I hope that you will not only have an
interest in the work of the Foundation but give us the participation
which I am very sure we want. That, in the end, is what counts.

Help us.

Mr. Mitchell: Thank you, Dr. Gilbreth. Thank you first for being here with us today on this occasion, thank you for the help you've given us over all these years, and thank you particularly for the thoughtful message that you have conveyed to us this morning.

You have heard from Dr. Angrist about The American Foundation for Management Research and its broad goals. I'm now going to ask Mr. Merritt L. Kastens to tell you about this AFMR Management Learning Center: its purposes, philosophy, and operation. Mr. Kastens is director of the Manager Learning Center. He has been a member of the staff of the Armour Research Foundation; a magazine editor; manager of planning and analysis for one of America's great corporations; and assistant director of Stanford Research Institute.

Address: "The AFMR Manager Learning Center: Its Purposes, Philosophy, and Operations"

MERRITT L. KASTENS
Director, AFMR Manager Learning Center

Let me begin by welcoming you here. You've been welcomed in the name of the American Management Association and The American Foundation for Management Research. I would like to welcome you in the name of the very many people who have made this occasion possible—who have made this building possible. I don't know how many of you know it specifically, but it was only last October that Mr. Appley and I stood very near this spot on which I'm standing today. We were in the middle of an alfalfa field, and we drove the first stakes to locate this building.

There were a great many people at that time who were very sure we could not build a 50,000-square-foot building in less than a year—not when we were going into the mid-upstate New York winter. But fortunately we found a lot of other people who were just as ignorant as we were. They didn't know it was impossible either. And so, a little more than seven months later, we moved into our offices in this building, and now the information and conference facilities are ready to operate.

I want to take this opportunity to express my appreciation to all the people who were involved. There's been a great personal dedication on the part of all the construction people—Don Burch, our general contractor; all his subcontractors; the craftsmen; the laborers; and their various organizations. I also want to acknowledge the substantial efforts of the Learning Center's staff because they have all made significant contributions to the design of the internal facilities of this building. And, of course, I want to acknowledge the support that we've received from the AMA staff here in Hamilton and in New York. They provided the substructure that permitted us all to go on with our special work for the Center.

These acknowledgments might very well raise a reasonable question: Why were we in such a hurry? Why were we so anxious to get a building designed and built in less than a year? Actually, to us the answer is quite simple. We saw a job to be done in and for the management community; we thought we knew a way to do the job, and we wanted to get at it just as fast as we possibly could.

For a number of years the people in AMA—that is, the staff and officers and the responsible people in the other AMA organizations—had been increasingly aware that there was a need for a technique that would make the existing know-how of management directly available to working management teams, some kind of direct injection-type technique. The traditional approach of presenting concepts and hoping to provide some new insights—and thus change attitudes which in turn might change some of the ways things are done and gradually change the actual direction of the enterprise —just was too slow and too inefficient to meet the pyramiding problems of the presently responsible managers.

This whole notion circulated within the AMA complex for a

number of years. The early researches that were sponsored by AFMR in universities across the country were aimed at this question and, at the same time, brought new insights into the need for the kind of technique we were thinking of. Research results from other sources, with which AMA had no direct connection, and the very pertinent observations of the people actually running AMA programs gradually began to give form and focus to this whole consideration.

Early in 1965, we in AFMR began to conduct some probing experiments to see if we couldn't develop a technique and approach that would serve this need. We experimented with new learning techniques, with new teaching techniques, with some of the old techniques, with case studies, with simulations, with games, and slowly the whole concept began to shape into a body of procedure. By the end of 1965 this form had begun to be reasonably recognizable, and by early 1966 the first version of what we've since come to call the "team learning process" had been outlined and full-scale experiments were undertaken with actual practicing management teams. By the middle of 1966—that is, the middle of last year—we had sufficient evidence and experience to feel that we had hit upon a technique that would work. That is to say, we had a technique by which we thought we could introduce the actual distillation of good management practice into a working situation, so that the accumulated skills and know-how could be made directly, immediately available.

Once we had that evidence, we decided to move ahead very quickly. The technique was very much dependent upon a certain physical environment, certain physical facilities, and so we immediately undertook to build an experimental facility about two miles north of here, adjacent to an existing AMA building known as the White House. We occupied that experimental facility and began to operate in it in September of last year. Some of the lessons we learned by operating there have been incorporated in the design of this building. We broke ground here in October, and we started experimenting in September. So you know that this building has been designed, in many respects, as we went along—all in the interest of speed. In fact, we operated in that experimental facility up until just a few weeks ago when we moved our furniture, so to speak, down to this building.

That's a very brief chronology of the history and development of this facility. Now, just what is this technique that we were so excited about, that we still are so excited about, and that gave us the confidence to take the very large step of erecting a building of this magnitude and complexity? Well, first of all, it's an action-oriented, problem-solving sort of technique. It's designed to respond directly to the real and current problems of the manager, of the *practicing* manager—the man who has the present responsibility. It accepts these problems in his terms, as he states them within his existing management framework, rather than trying to translate them into the terms of some sort of theoretical structure. It's oriented toward an action: what we call an operational change, what the behavioral scientists call a behavioral change rather than a conceptual or attitude change. We didn't invent this theory; we did not discover here that you can change behavior directly and then allow the changed behavior to feed back into an attitudinal change. But we're very much impressed with the efficacy of the technique for our particular purposes.

An essential characteristic of our process is that it is a *team* learning process. We take full advantage of the existing structure of management. We work with it as a social unit, with its authority and its history, whatever aberrations and distortions may exist in it. We work with and within that social unit so that when we do come to an action end, that action immediately constitutes a change in social behavior. It isn't a question of changing *individual* behavior; rather, we have the advantage of the social momentum that's created by working within an existing structure.

We call our process, you may have noticed, a *learning* process, and we do that rather self-consciously to emphasize the fact that the active role is that of the learner—of the manager. We sometimes say that by the time a man gets to be president you can't teach him very much any more, but he *does* learn. Thus we feel that the manager who comes here will himself draw out of our various resources those things that he needs and can use and will put them into a useful pattern.

This learning process, in short, takes one step further the longstanding AMA credo that working managers learn best by observing critically the successful practice of other working managers.

The resources of the Learning Center are organized into substance centers. Each of these substance centers undertakes to assemble the most comprehensive record possible of actual successful practice in some area of management responsibility. The record is inherent in the observations and experiences of a resident staff of management specialists; after all, the human brain is still a great retrieval system. But this biological system is augmented by a highly codified electronic information storage and retrieval system. The system already contains information from literally thousands of organizations—detailed, explicit, factual information about how they approach certain aspects of their management procedure. The system is indexed in depth so that this experience, this record of successful performance, can be available in small units which enable the learner to see it in detail.

We don't believe that a complex management system can very often be taken and moved whole from one organization to another. The transplant usually doesn't take. An organization needs a management system that responds to its own particular history, its personality, and its degree of sophistication. But it is possible to assemble a successful system from a mosaic of the detailed practices of other companies, put together to correspond to the peculiar operational characteristics of the new organization.

It can readily be inferred from these comments that we do not believe in formula solutions to management problems. We do not have any "black boxes" to sell, nor do we have any pat solutions on the shelf. We do feel that the record of successful performance by professionally managed companies that we have here, if approached in a valid conceptual framework, can lead—will lead inevitably—to a productive force for management action which must improve management practice. But again, you see, it has to be drawn out of the resources by the learner, not imposed by an "expert" teacher.

In practice, the essence of this process is to take a company's operating management team, the top policy group, bring its members into a situation almost completely free of distractions, and enable them—sometimes, it seems, even force them—to concentrate their attention unremittingly on the management problem that they themselves have recognized. During this forced concentration—in this "pressure cooker" atmosphere, if you like—they will have direct and virtually instantaneous access to the experience and the conclusions of other practicing managers who have faced comparable problems in the real world.

The role of the Center's staff is to provide guidance, to play the devil's advocate, to make suggestions, to call attention to existing solutions that have worked in the past, and in general to maintain the deliberately induced intensification of the management process which is, in fact, what occurs in the learning rooms here. The Center's staff does not advocate. It does not advise. But at the same time we feel very confident in assuring managers who come here as a company team that when they leave, when they complete the process, they will have decided upon a complete course of management action which is immediately *usable* within their ongoing operational situation.

There's never any question of acquiring a principle in a learning situation and then having to go somewhere else—back home, back to the job—and figure out how to apply that principle. The work of application is done here before the team ever leaves. This is perhaps the most significant part of our process. It's significant, also, that the application takes place virtually unconsciously. The team members are not aware of making the transition from concept to action. They move directly into the action phase. Principle and practice are completely integrated.

I would like to emphasize again what Dr. Angrist has already said: that whenever we talk of management, managers, or a management team, we're thinking of a function that must be fulfilled whenever human beings work together to achieve results. Management is not a matter of profit or no profit, industry or institution, political body or what have you. Our initial sessions, admittedly, have all been with industrial organizations for the very simple reason that these are the people whom we know the best and who know us the best. However, we're looking forward to working with people from all kinds of organizations: public agencies, welfare and cultural groups, political entities, labor unions—whoever has a management responsibility or a management problem. This is not to say that we think we can do everything for everybody, be all things to all men immediately. However, we're optimistic that we have here a technique of general applicability.

Our learning sessions, in the strict sense, are structured. Indeed, the process itself requires a good deal of structuring, and very large information banks are needed to enable it to function. Our initial programs have been limited to strategic long-range corporate planning and to managerial manpower planning. We're just now activating a program in management control, and we're in the process of developing programs in the areas of executive performance standards and operational planning. We're also just beginning an investigation of strategic long-range planning in the collegiate situation. The initial research is being carried on under the auspices of Colgate University, with financial support from an AFMR grant and program guidance from the Learning Center's staff. We hope this will result in a collegiate counterpart of our present program in corporate planning. And we'll initiate programs in other fields—with specific kinds of management and specific kinds of organizations to be managed—just as fast as we can formulate plans and recruit staff.

Our long-range hope is that the Learning Center will become a place where managers at all levels, in all kinds of organizations, can come with real problems; work with the greatest concentration of resources, pertinent to those problems, that we can muster; and develop practical solutions which they can then take home and apply directly. This is a large dream. We know it. But there's no question that a demand exists for this kind of institution and that, at the present time, the demand is not being met. We believe we have at least the beginning of a technique that can meet it.

We're part of a research foundation, and we will always be changing, experimenting, improving. We'll expect to draw new knowledge, new ideas, from many sources—from the behavioral sciences, from the educational hardware and software people, from the information-processing systems which are developing so rapidly these days, and of course from the developing science of management itself. However, we will hew close to the line of the problem-solving, real-time, on-line kind of approach.

We want to be truly an applied research operation here. We're concerned with helping the manager with his current problems. These problems will change; we know that, and we know we will have to change with them.

What they will be in the year 2000 no one, of course, knows for sure. We'll hear a lot of ideas in the next day and a half as to just what the developments may be in the remaining years of the century. But I think we're safe in assuming that management will have to be more precise and, at the same time, more flexible and more knowledgeable. The margin for error will undoubtedly be greatly reduced. The tolerance for archaic management techniques, I'm sure, will disappear. We definitely expect that by the year 2000 our understanding of the management process will have become much more explicit than it is today and, presumably, the record of successful management will be much more complete.

Through its research activities, AFMR should contribute to this rationalization of management, and certainly it should be instrumental in maintaining and organizing the record of successful management practice. Its role, as we see it, is that of a major pipeline or conduit through which our developing understanding and knowledge of the management process—management as Dr. Gilbreth defined it—will be transmitted into the working situation and applied to the current problems of the men who carry the responsibility for implementing the dreams and plans of mankind. This *is* the essence of management.

MR. MITCHELL: I hope that you now are beginning to get a little idea of the concept that is in back of this place and how we are proceeding to implement that concept. I'm sure that before these two days are over you will have a still better idea.

This concludes our morning session.

Introduction

DR. ARTHUR W. ANGRIST
AFMR Vice President and Managing Director

All of you are aware, I am sure, that the complexity of our society has been increasing rapidly, especially since the end of World War II, and it is safe to assume that this trend will continue in the years ahead. By the year 2000 this complexity may well have reached a point where much of our national educational resource will be devoted, in one way or another, to preparing our citizenry to cope with it.

Our educators are thus on the threshold of great change, as is the management environment outside the world of education. What relationship will exist between these two worlds in the year 2000? What will happen, for example, to the ideals of the liberal arts colleges in that highly technological society? Will interest in the humanities disappear as an influence on modern life, or will the old ideal survive and perhaps have an even greater impact on the modern manager?

Our first speaker this afternoon will be addressing his thoughts to "The Impact of Higher Education upon the Management Environment in the Year 2000." He is knowledgeable about both higher education and management. As president of Colgate University he manages an important unit in what is now said to be our second largest industry—education. He has also had extensive experience in another large organization—the U.S. Government.

Vincent MacDowell Barnett, born in Whittier, California, attended the University of California at Los Angeles, where he received both his bachelor's and his master's degree. He received his Ph.D. from Harvard University in 1938. In 1939 Dr. Barnett joined the faculty of Williams College, and in 1946 he was named chairman of the political science department, serving in that capacity until 1963. During that period he was dean of the college (1957–1958), chairman of the Graduate Center for Economic Development, and director of overseas projects. On February 1, 1963, Dr. Barnett became president of Colgate University, that other "learning center" across town from us that a group of energetic Baptists established 148 years ago. They've done rather well with it since then, and we certainly hope to follow their good example.

Dr. Barnett has also had a distinguished career in government. During the latter part of World War II he served as vice chairman of the War Production Board Requirements Committee. He then returned to Williams to teach. After the war his special knowledge and administrative experience were called into use as assistant chief to the U.S. Aid Mission to Italy, as deputy chief of the Mutual Security Agency Mission to Italy, and as economic counselor to the American Embassy in Rome. In 1960 the Department of State awarded him the highly regarded Superior Service Award for his work.

Address: "The Impact of Higher Education upon the Management Environment in the Year 2000"

DR. VINCENT M. BARNETT, JR.
President, Colgate University

It may have occurred to you that university presidents must love to make speeches, since they seem to be doing it all the time. Lest you take this occasion as one more bit of evidence to support your erroneous theories, let me tell you I tried my best to get out of this one. Unfortunately for you, I was unsuccessful. Having fortified myself with a number of wise sayings—such as "A closed mouth gathers no feet" and "Nothing is often a good thing to say and always a clever thing to say"—I had decided to make no speeches this summer. I even got out of town. Then came the one invitation I could not really decline. So here I am, contributing again to the regrettable image of the loquacious university president. I guess we just have to be thick-skinned about these things. I am comforted by the advice which Sam Goldwyn gave on how to deal with motion picture critics: "Don't pay any attention to them; don't even ignore them." As for the speech, once you have started it's like an airplane engine—no matter how terrible it sounds, you have to go on.

The dedication of the Manager Learning Center of The American Foundation for Management Research is an event of considerable importance from several points of view. It is, of course, most immediately and most obviously a significant day in the life of the village of Hamilton and the surrounding community. The contribution which AMA has made to this area seems now to be assured and magnified for a long time into the future. Our visitors will, I am sure, forgive me if I mention this first, but I think it appropriate to note that the local community both appreciates and welcomes this new undertaking as a further evidence of its friendly and fruitful relationship with AMA.

The occasion also marks a significant development for Colgate University. For a number of years there has been a special relationship between AMA and Colgate, deriving not only from the common location in Hamilton but more especially from the fact that Larry Appley once taught at Colgate and now serves as a highly valued member of its board of trustees. The University has benefited from AMA's presence and looks forward now to an increasingly productive relationship through the activities of the Manager Learning Center. This cooperation has already begun through the establishment of a joint project through which the University and the Center will undertake a path-breaking study of the possible applications of the technological resources of the Center to the problems of institutions of higher learning.

Let me be just a bit more specific on this point. As the colleges and universities of this country look toward the year 2000, they face a number of diverse and challenging and sometimes disturbing problems. Many people have prepared lists of such problems, and I have my own list. I think you would find on every thoughtful list the identification of two major problems. One is the necessity to do a better job in managing the resources of the institution to achieve its educational ends. This is largely, though not wholly, a financial problem. It may give the appearance of being a simple problem of management. But the extent to which educational institutions can or should be run on classical management principles is a matter of great debate and much controversy—sometimes bitter. Some say the business operations of a university can and should be more highly professionalized from a management point of view. Others say there is no reason why the same process cannot be extended to the academic program. Still others disagree with one or both of these propositions. But it is perhaps fair to say that no one really knows, on the basis of careful and objective study, just what are the possible benefits and the possible limitations of a more professional management approach in the operation of institutions of higher learning. I myself would guess that there are some real benefits to be derived but that there are also some very substantial dangers. In any case, it is about time we found out, or tried to. Colgate's joint project with the Manager Learning Center is designed to be at least a first step in this direction.

The second great need on everybody's list would be the requirement for more and better institutional research and the relation of this to the planning function of the university. The joint project, drawing on the technological resources of the Center, will address itself also to this problem. Colgate expects to benefit directly as an institution from this project, but it is the hope and expectation of the co-sponsors that the findings will also be of value to many institutions throughout the country.

Hence, from a broader point of view, the dedication of the Center in this community is an event which holds great promise for two other communities which reach far beyond this pleasant valley. One is the community of higher education in the United States, and the other is the nationwide (indeed worldwide) community of professional managers.

And this brings me, not entirely by accident, to the topic to which I have been invited to address the bulk of my remarks today. It is, in fact, the intersection of these two communities in the year

2000 or, as the program has it, "The Impact of Higher Education on the Management Environment in the Year 2000."

If I really address myself to this topic, I will have to make some guesses about the character and shape of higher education in this country in the year 2000. This is a most difficult assignment. On looking over the program, however, I see that several others are faced with the same kind of task, and I suppose my crystal ball is no cloudier than theirs.

Predicting is a dangerous and frustrating game. It is much easier to say what *should* happen or what *must* happen in higher education by the 21st century than it is to say what *will* happen. There are articles and speeches galore on the prerequisites for the survival of private colleges, for example, or on the broad agenda of things that must be done in higher education by the end of the century. There are fewer serious efforts to predict what the pattern will in fact be. Yet I think my topic requires me to try. I wouldn't dare do this on one of my gloomy days, because our culture requires that anyone in a position of leadership be outwardly optimistic and confident of the future (even at the cost of basic honesty) if he is to exercise a reasonably effective leadership role. Fortunately, this is not one of my gloomy days.

One way to predict anything is to project present trends. Obviously, this is not an infallible method, but in the absence of better tools it may be the best one we have. I remember a friend of mine, a lawyer by profession, who served in the Air Force in World War II as a meteorologist. He was at an Air Force base on the Foggia plain in southern Italy. As he observed the weather forecasting for the flights taking off from Foggia, he was forcibly struck by the imprecision of the results. So he ran his own little experiment. He would set down the daily weather forecast arrived at by the latest scientific method using the most advanced instruments and the best technology available. Then he would set down alongside it a forecast based on the simple proposition that tomorrow's weather would be much like today's. Then, after the event, he would set down the actual weather. He was much amused to discover that his batting average with his simple rule-of-thumb forecasts was somewhat higher than that of the official forecasts. This might reasonably have indicated the abolition of the meteorological unit, but I gather he did not suggest this to his commanding officer. In the event that there are any offended meteo-

rologists in the audience, let me hasten to add that I am sure technological advances since then have increased the precision of professional forecasting.

My point is that in the absence of highly refined tools for forecasting one is almost constrained to begin with a projection of present trends. If one were to do that in the field of higher education, I
think he might conclude that by the year 2000 our system of higher
education would reveal most if not all of the following characteristics:

1. Almost all young Americans will seek and receive some
   form of higher education beyond the high school level.

2. This education may not take place entirely on college campuses as now conceived, although colleges and universities
   will continue to be deeply involved in it.

3. Continuing education for adults will bulk much larger
   than it does now, both on the campuses of educational institutions and through learning and information-retrieval
   centers located elsewhere.

4. Formal higher education will continue to be a monopoly
   of the colleges and universities, but more and more educational activities will be undertaken by business corporations, governmental agencies, television networks, and the
   like, with or without university connections.

5. A much higher proportion of students in the formal educational system will be enrolled in public institutions. Perhaps as much as 85 or 90 percent of the total student enroll-
   ment will be in clearly public institutions as contrasted to
   private institutions.

6. The line of demarcation between public and private institutions will have become a very fuzzy one, with all so-called
   private institutions relying to some significant degree on
   public support from state or federal sources in a variety of
   ways.

7. Although many institutions in the shadow zone between
   private and public will have lost some substantial portion
   of their autonomy, there will remain a small minority of
   strong private institutions capable of leadership and innovation outside the constraints of the publicly supported
   system.

8. Although the pressures toward excessive and premature specialization will be stronger than ever, there will remain in most undergraduate institutions a healthy commitment to the liberal arts and to the preparation of the generalist so badly needed by an increasingly specialized society; and there will be an increasing interest in the liberally educated generalist both on the part of government and on the part of business.

9. The great public universities will have become even larger and more prestigious (although the physical pattern will have moved more toward decentralization, "cluster colleges," and multiple campuses), and these institutions will have become virtual partners with government and business in "the knowledge industry."

10. The teaching process, which has remained essentially unchanged since the appearance of the printed book, will have altered markedly for the vast majority of students, becoming more mechanized and impersonal; but there will still be highly personal and individualized teaching for an élite defined by ability and motivation, whether in the smaller institutions or in honors-type programs in the larger institutions.

Some of you may feel that I have allowed my hopes to color these predictions. And you may be right. In my view there are some clear imperatives for higher education in the next 30 years or so, and I have perhaps been guilty of assuming that what is needed will somehow be brought about. I do plead guilty to a belief in the efficacy of human effort and to a faith that we can, within limits, fashion our destinies. But, whether as pure predictions or as goals, I should like to comment on a few of the points I have listed.

I choose to speak of three survivals: the survival of the university as such, the survival of the private institution, and the survival of the liberal arts educational concept. Since they have all been pronounced more or less moribund on numerous occasions, my assumption that they will still be on the scene by the year 2000 may need some elaboration beyond the dubious expectation that tomorrow's weather will be much like today's.

Pessimism about the future of the university as such derives primarily from the fact that the community expects so much from the university and falls so far short of providing the resources necessary to meet those expectations.

If we were to try to make even an incomplete catalogue of the ways in which the community expects its universities to behave, we would get a long list. The community expects the university to act as a producer of the skills and techniques needed by society; it expects the university to act as social critic; it expects the university to act as a partner with government and business not only in research but also in the administration of various enterprises. It expects the university to act as the discoverer of new knowledge; it expects the university to create a public-spirited citizenry; it expects the university to act as a setter of standards of excellence in all walks of life. It expects the university to provide the long view on the evolving aims and goals of society; it expects the university to act as the conservator of the best of the past; it expects the university to act as innovator and experimenter; it expects the university to inspire a respect for true creativity and to be a source of much of our creative activity. And it expects the university to provide formal classroom instruction and organized education both at the undergraduate level and in the various professional and technical specialities—organized, formal education which will, among other things, prepare tomorrow's leaders for the year 2000. It does not seem to give any clear indication of which of these expectations should be assigned the highest priority, nor does it give any indication that it is prepared, as a society, to finance them all to the degree which would permit them all to be effectively carried out at the same time.

From this point of view one of the greatest problems of the modern university is the allocation of limited resources to the various kinds of demands pressed upon it by the community. Under these circumstances it is not surprising that the balance which is kept among these various activities may from time to time be distorted by the availability of funds from particular sources with particular objectives attached.

Few university presidents would deny that if their entire income to be budgeted for annual operations were available to them without any restrictions of this kind, the pattern of activities of the university would probably be substantially different in the future from what it is today. Nor would they deny that the timing of new undertakings, whether in terms of physical plant or in terms of new programs, might very well be considerably different if the funds that became available for such things were to be allocated in terms of the university's own judgment as to priorities.

I suppose it might also be generally agreed that the American community does not provide enough of its total resources for higher education and that those it does provide sometimes result in uneven and distorted progress toward goals which the university might better approximate if resources were more adequately available.

If we are to make guesses about the future, the safest policy would be to assume that this is likely to continue to be the case. But I personally believe that a more nearly adequate total level of financial support for institutions of higher education will be forthcoming over the years ahead, although I also suspect that a growing proportion of this support will be made available by the community through the use of the taxing power and the appropriation of public revenues for the purpose.

Private support of higher education, although increasing in absolute terms, is declining significantly as a proportion of the total despite vigorous efforts to induce corporate and other private donors to increase their support. I suspect that these efforts will continue to bear some fruit, but that they will be outstripped by the response of state legislatures and, increasingly, the Federal Government.

Not all of the major changes induced by external forces have been the result of a growing affinity between industry and the universities or between government and the universities. Another significant influence, and to some extent an offsetting one, has been the emergence to importance in recent years of the large private foundations. As catalysts they have had a tremendous impact. It can be said with considerable justice that they have been the main instruments in the reform of medical education, in the introduction of interdisciplinary studies, and in the involvement of universities in world affairs on a large scale. The problem of maintaining a healthy undergraduate science program in the liberal arts colleges is a vital one to which constructive foundation attention is being given. I have no doubt that the effect of foundation activity has been remarkable in relation to the amount of resources actually involved and has been most beneficial.

The universities as such will survive, therefore, not simply because they are learning to adapt to the multiple demands of society,

but because there are certain tasks for which they are uniquely qualified. Sir Eric Ashby, noted English educator, rejects the proposition
that the university's survival depends primarily on adaptation to outside forces over which it has no real control. He notes that there are
tasks for which only the universities themselves can take the initiative, tasks which will not in all likelihood be forced upon them by
the outside world. Among these are the cultivation of excellence and
the preservation of the right to be different and the right to be dangerous.

Society as a whole cannot be expected to force the universities to
do any of these things, but Ashby believes that the universities themselves will continue to fulfill these roles. Democracies, he says, will
never nurture élites, but the university will continue to stress the
importance of the élite of excellence even in the midst of a rapidly
expanding effort to generate education for the whole society. It is the
universities which must be sure that the slogan "More means worse"
is not necessarily true of education. American universities, says
Ashby, must firmly grasp the responsibility for the nurture of excellence within the framework of mass higher education. American universities are ahead of others in this endeavor, but no one has yet
found a really reliable formula. This, according to Ashby, is the main
task for the next century for those concerned with higher education.

The right to remain different and the right to remain dangerous
are not likely to be forced upon the universities from the outside, either. The forces in society as a whole are more likely to push the university in the direction of conformity and of performance as the
complacent producers of the techniques and skills which society
thinks it requires. The technocratic state, according to Sir Eric, will
resent dangerous ideas; and all new ideas, if they are important
enough, are dangerous. "Universities must remain places where new
ideas are cherished, where individualism is welcome, where anyone
who has any of the precious fire of originality is encouraged to think
'otherwise.'"

It is for many of these same reasons that I think the private institutions of higher learning must and will survive. Surely it is the private colleges and universities which are best able to be different, to
innovate, and to nurture the élite of excellence within a framework
of mass education. I am convinced that business management, that
the private sector of the economy in general, indeed that society as a

whole will see this and respond to it—despite the ambiguous evidence of the record so far.

As for the survival of the liberal arts, the increasing specialization of our world and the increasing impact of technology will make this more—not less—essential by the year 2000. The university in its strictly service function to society will be more and more pressed to produce the specialists and technicians obviously required. The university in its leadership role will have to see to it that the community gets the generalists it will need in an even more vital sense.

The big decisions which determine the fate of nations and quite possibly the future of mankind on this planet are in the hands of generalists. To be sure, the problem of how to produce a properly educated generalist has not yet been solved by the universities. I quote Ashby from a 1964 address at the Cornell Centennial Celebration:

> I do not think that universities, American or British, are satisfied with the education they give to the man who is to become a generalist. Some believe he should have a rigorously specialist training in some field which he then abandons for life. Others believe he should have a synoptic acquaintance with the ways of thinking of humanists, social scientists, and natural scientists. And I suppose there are still a few antique persons who cling to the view that generalists need no higher education at all. We can with some confidence prescribe the *minutiae* of curricula for doctors, physicists, and lawyers. The unpalatable fact is that we have no such confidence in prescribing curricula for men who will become presidents of industries, newspaper editors, senior civil servants, or Congressmen.

Here Sir Eric echoes a point made by the late Adlai Stevenson. "Radio, television, jet transport," said Mr. Stevenson, "have condensed the world within the confines of a church parish. Our universities have not yet responded adequately to this consequence of technology. The response required is not technological: it is humane."

The response to which both Ashby and Stevenson refer will have to be found in a reaffirmation of the values and a renewal of the vigor of the liberal arts as the basic educational experience for leaders in all walks of life. And I would like to suggest that this is one of the major aspects of the impact of higher education on the management environment in the remaining years of this century. The best managers in an increasingly complex society characterized by a bewildering rate of change will be those who have had a sound liberal arts education, whatever its professional or technical overlay, and who through organized programs or through self-development have kept abreast of the changing context of thought and knowledge in which their own decisions are made and tested. And the best managers will be those who are able to recruit and retain colleagues with such backgrounds and perspective.

The present danger is that this will be overlooked in the pressure for specialization—including, if we are not careful, the specialization of the professional manager as such.

Of all the many roles which the community expects the university to fulfill, or which the community ought to expect the university to fulfill, that having to do with the basic attitude and outlook of the broadly educated man is undoubtedly the most important for the long-run survival of civilization. I like the description provided by Dr. Peter Odegard in a 1965 address at the University of Pittsburgh. He said:

> The educated man, as virtually every study shows, is more tolerant of ambiguity, less xenophobic, less given to anxiety, more under-standing and hence more tolerant of cultural and political differ-ences, less likely to appear in a divorce court, on the police blotter, or in a mental institution. He is less likely to be taken captive by ideological clichés or to give way to fantasy in defiance of, or in-difference to, the facts of life. He is more likely to believe in the efficacy of political participation to effect rational changes in the social order and more likely to prefer peaceful persuasion to violence in bringing about changes in the political power structure. He is less likely to suffer from what psychologists call *anomie,* i.e., social, cultural, or political alienation. He is more at home in his family, his community, his country, and a pluralistic universe—more stable and contented but at the same time more hopeful of the future and less fearful of change. He is, in a word, more civilized.

Perhaps, by the year 2000, such a description will apply more ac-curately to the substantial majority of our population. It may even apply more accurately to our professional managers and our profes-sional educators.

One of the wisest and most articulate voices in the field of educa-tion in recent times is that of John W. Gardner, now Secretary of Health, Education and Welfare and previously president of the

Carnegie Corporation. In an essay written before he assumed his Cabinet post and published in the annual report of the Corporation in 1965, Mr. Gardner warned business and education alike of a growing fallacy that the world of the future "does not need leaders, only experts." Many managers in business and government, he said, are falling victim to the "modern art" of "how to reach a decision without really deciding." The abdication of the leadership function in favor of the internal clearance process—that is, seeking a consensus of experts—is a reflection of the loss of confidence in leaders. On the other hand, he added, the inability on the part of many top-level executives to understand society's needs in broad terms is weakening the private sector of leadership and will result in the increasing turnover of responsibility to the government.

At the same time, Mr. Gardner charged educational institutions with immunizing potential leaders by what he called a powerful anti-leadership vaccine. "Students are given the impression that corporation presidents, politicians, and college presidents are corrupted by power, compromise, and status-seeking—in contrast to the integrity of scholars." As a consequence of this negative image of leadership, the "academic world appears to be approaching a point at which everyone will want to educate the technical expert who advises the leader or the intellectual who stands off and criticizes the leader, but no one will want to educate the leader himself." The various aids to decision making, such as questionnaires, statistical systems, cost-benefit analyses, information processing devices, computers, and the like, are all valuable tools but can never replace the ultimate human judgment. The educational system and the business and governmental organizations must somehow produce and find ways of recognizing the broadly trained potential manager who has the perspective and the confidence which will enable him to make the necessary leadership decisions in a complicated and changing world.

Similarly, the modern university must discover the extent to which sound management practices tested in business may be applicable to educational institutions. Let me say at once that I am sure there are certain areas in which so-called management techniques are out of place in a university. These are probably for the most part on the strictly academic side of the institution's operation. The recent example of a Middle Western institution—which shall be nameless—that tried to apply so-called business concepts across the board suggests that ultimately such an effort is likely to be unsuccessful financially as well as educationally. Sol Linowitz, until recently a top executive at Xerox and currently a U.S. ambassador, as well as a trustee at both the University of Rochester and Hamilton College, once wrote an article with a title that says it all in a few words: "A Liberal Arts College Is Not a Railroad." His conclusion was that American business and industry "will have to understand that much of liberal education which is urgently worth saving cannot be justified on a dollars-and-cents basis." But all this is not to say that there are no areas in which the universities would benefit from more professional and more effective management practices. It seems to me they have an obligation to determine what these areas are (the typical business operations of the university are, of course, a prime candidate) and an obligation to see to what degree the distilled experience of business management can be helpful.

I would hope, though I would not be so hardy as to predict, that the year 2000 will see a much closer working relationship between business and higher education, flowing from a substantial diminution of the mutual distrust which seems to color much of the attitude of each toward the other in the 1960's. Higher education will never allow itself to be dominated by business criteria nor wish itself to be judged primarily by standards of business efficiency. Business will never fully understand the pluralism of the university, with its loosely organized and seemingly inefficient procedures and practices. But the pressures of the future will require that each seek more vigorously to understand the other, and out of the search for understanding may come a realization of a greater community of interest and purpose than either would suspect today. I am sure this is one of the goals of the American Management Association and of The American Foundation for Management Research, which is but another reason I am pleased to be taking part in these proceedings.

DR. ANGRIST: Dr. Barnett, you have provided us with a number of stimulating and interesting ideas, and we're grateful to you for sharing them with us.

Opening Remarks

DR. ARTHUR W. ANGRIST
AFMR Vice President and Managing Director

The field of information retrieval is one which is growing by leaps and bounds. The technology and its application, the thinking and findings that are being brought to bear on this subject area are most stimulating, if not somewhat bewildering, to many of us who are not actively engaged in the field. There have been many, many new developments in devices for transmitting information, and we often find ourselves with much more information being received than we ever dreamed existed. It is hard for me to tell, as a layman, what the situation will be in the year 2000, but I'm sure that our panel members will be able to present some interesting ideas regarding this important area.

Our panel chairman, who will interrogate and introduce the members of his panel, is Mr. Henry Boettinger, assistant comptroller of the American Telephone and Telegraph Company. Mr. Boettinger obtained his engineering degree from Johns Hopkins University; he did advanced work at the University of Michigan in physics and studied economics at New York University Graduate School. He served as an Air Force navigator in World War II, as well as in the Signal Corps. Mr. Boettinger joined the Bell System in Maryland in 1948 and served in many of its companies before becoming assistant comptroller of AT&T in 1962.

Reflecting his dual interest in engineering and economics, as well as in education, Mr. Boettinger is a member of the Visiting Committee of the School of Engineering Sciences at Johns Hopkins University and a member of the New York University Committee on Education Policy, Graduate School of Business Administration. He is an author and a very articulate and stimulating thinker.

Panel: "The State of Information Retrieval and Data Processing in the Year 2000 and Its Implications for Management"

Chairman:

HENRY M. BOETTINGER
Assistant Comptroller, American Telephone and Telegraph Company

Panel Members:

DR. C. W. CHURCHMAN
Associate Director, Space Sciences Laboratory, and Professor of Business Administration, University of California (Berkeley)

WILLIAM T. KNOX
Vice President, Information Services, McGraw-Hill Company

NORMAN J. REAM
Special Assistant to the Secretary of the Navy

Introduction by Mr. Boettinger

One of the problems associated with dedicating a center such as this is that we are forced to consider that we are in an age of transition—and that this age of transition has been with us for a long time. It probably started in the Garden of Eden when Eve came to Adam and said, "Adam, old boy, I've had a taste of this beautiful apple," and he said, "Eve, my dear, we're in an age of transition."

To some extent the folklore and mythology of Western culture are full of what happens to people who pick up new things. Prometheus got in trouble by stealing fire from heaven, and Faust—well, you all know what happened to him. And now here we are as panel members proposing to make you sit through some more talk about "that hardware stuff." I'm afraid that we have a real smörgasbord for you, although that, of course, is a matter of taste.

I would like, however, to compare the relationship of the hardware to the problem as Lewis Mumford does in his book *The Myth of the Machine*. Mumford says that the brain has the same relationship to the mind as a phonograph record has to the music that's on it. In other words, if you ask, "What's on that record?" the engineer says, "There're a lot of grooves—20,000 to the inch. It took a lot of work." But another man says, "I think it's Beethoven's Ninth."

Now, they are both accurate. To some extent the problem facing us, and the one we're discussing, is: What is the state of information retrieval techniques? We're talking about the microgrooves, but I'm sure we would come much closer to your particular problems if we were to talk about the music that's going to be on there. In line with this, I will quote from Thorstein Veblen—and it is a certain measure of the sophistication of management that I can take that risk. He says, "Immutable conduct and progressively changing conditions result in a logical muddle." You can't argue with that!

What we're going to have to concern ourselves with, then, is both how we can take account of both progressively changing conditions and what our proper type of conduct is to be. It's very fortunate, under the circumstances, that at this point I am able to introduce to you a distinguished panel. The approach we'd like to use here, since we're dealing with one hard-core diamond that has many facets, is to have each of the gentlemen make his 15- to 20-minute presentation. In that way we can be sure of getting a triangulation of our problem. Then, after that, we will entertain questions—if you're still here.

One of these distinguished men, the one on my right, is Wes Churchman. Wes is now professor of business administration and also associate director of the Space Science Laboratory of the University of California at Berkeley. He began as a philosopher, having been an editor in the philosophy of science and in management science, as well as vice president of the American Academy for the Advancement of Science.

Wes has also been a founding seminal thinker in operations research. With Russell L. Ackoff and E. Leonard Arnoff he wrote *Introduction to Operations Research,* a basic classic in the field. In addition he has to his credit books dealing with the philosophy of science and ethics, with the theory of experimental inference and methods of inquiry, prediction, and optimal decision. He currently heads a large project, at the University of California, which is studying the management of research in industry and government.

I. Presentation by Dr. Churchman

I'll be addressing myself to the music on the records, not the microgrooves, since my interest is mainly in the philosophy of information systems. I shall, in fact, try to say something about how modern technology might or might not assist in making information systems into something more compatible with the management process.

I'd like to begin with a brief summary of my understanding of the past decade and a half, or two decades, with respect both to information systems and to mathematical models. Very briefly, I think it's fair to say that in the period from 1950 to 1967 there has been a modicum of success on the part of mathematical model builders in portraying some very important management processes. I would say that by 1955 operations researchers had established their ability to look at production problems with a good deal of competence; by 1960 they had established their ability to look at financial problems; and by 1965 their ability to look at marketing and, to some extent, budgeting. And possibly by 1970 the mathematical model builders will be having a modicum of success in corporate planning.

But, in a very true sense, the solutions of the mathematical model builders have been quite circumscribed. This is mainly because we have had to slice off one piece of reality and examine it more or less in isolation from the rest in order for our model building to be feasible. Hence I think it's doubtful whether any technique at the present time—model building or whatever—is capable of grasping enough of reality to guarantee that management will really improve the system it manages. In other words, at this stage in the 1960's we haven't a technology of any kind—in old-fashioned management principles or modern mathematical model building—that really grasps enough of the real system to assure us that what we are changing constitutes a real improvement.

If we turn to information systems, I think we can see the same theme there. The information that's in present-day information systems is specific and detailed. It tells about some very specific pieces of reality. But what I think the manager of today, and of the year 2000, is going to need more and more is not just these snapshots that tell him something about a piece or slice of reality but a picture of what reality is like. Then he can sense, vis-à-vis a given plan, what life will be like living with that plan.

In terms of the development of international plans, or multinational companies, what seems to be very desperately needed is a realistic presentation to the manager about what life will be like when the company acquires foreign subsidiaries. What the information systems of today have, for the multinational company, is statistical data on the growth and decline of foreign markets, trends in financial patterns, inflation or depression in foreign countries, and so on. None of all this, however, touches the realities the manager will face when he begins to manage something as complex as a multinational company.

Will it be possible in the few decades ahead of us to develop into our information systems more of a sense of the reality of a system in addition to the detailed specifics of information? That's what I want to address myself to—these possibilities. I'm not going to forecast that by the year 2000 we will have an information system that is realistic in my sense. I *am* going to speculate about what we might try to do—that is, suggest some ideas that might be appropriate for aiming in that direction.

The key word here is "story." We need the ability to tell stories about the future—the kind of thing Herman Kahn did when he wrote his scenarios. We need to be able to put some alternative stories about what the future is going to be into information systems for managers, and then determine what their plans will be like when these systems are realized in the future.

In order to do this, instead of looking at information systems as a kind of up-to-date rapid transmittal of data that are already being handled on a manual basis, we also need to bring into the information retrieval area the inventive mind—the mind that's really asking, "Isn't there something we can do beyond the mere accumulation of bits and pieces of information in statistical form?" Well, my suggestion is that management information systems should have the ability to tell challenging, relevant, and plausible alternative stories about the consequences of possible management decisions.

Each of these words is important. Management information systems ought to be *challenging*; therefore, they oughtn't to be extrapolations—the dull kind of thing that most of us do when we're forecasting. They should really make us object sometimes. Management information systems should be *relevant*—highly relevant—to the manager; that is, they ought to mean so much to him that he is more than anxious to follow them. They need to be *plausible* in the sense that from where he stands in 1967 what is said about 1984 or 2000 doesn't look ridiculous. And they ought to offer alternatives—that is, there ought to be more than one story about what's going to happen.

Every plan that management and its planners develop, including the present *status quo* plan, has a story in back of it. For any candidate plan that a manager is considering, this story should be made explicit. It may not be a story that we have the technological ability to prove objectively true, but there is a story there.

For example, we have just heard a speech on the future of institutions of higher education. There's a story behind the notion that independent liberal arts education should continue to exist, and it's that story that ought to be told as explicitly as possible. But the counterstory should be told also, and that is the story about what reality with the whole system will be like if it's no longer appropriate to have independent educational institutions. There is such a story, and it can be told. And I think it ought to be told to today's and tomorrow's educators.

For every plan, then, there is the appropriate story that goes along to support it. And then there is the story that goes along with the counterplan—the challenger—so that none of our planning will take place in the context of a dream, which I think is the deadly sin of planners. We are not looking for plans that everyone will agree to; we are looking for plans whose every alternative we have inspected thoroughly in all the honesty and fierceness that we can. After we have done this, looked at the various stories that go along with our plans and counterplans—that is, when we have challenged our plan and our concepts to the fullest—perhaps we will be in a position to make our judgment. That's what I would like to see the information system of the year 2000 do for the manager.

I can imagine that—with the capability of the computer, the skills of the journalist and the dramatist, and all the other disciplines that would have to get into this act—such a briefing might be a vivid graphic display. The manager would be exposed to alternative stories, and connected with each story would be a specific plan of action. And it would be up to the manager to decide which of those stories he appreciated most. (The word "appreciate" here means to value highest.) What I'm looking for, in short, is the maximization of the manager's opportunity, through the information system, to use his appreciative skills in the most effective way possible.

MR. BOETTINGER: I'm sure I saw some feverish note taking there, so we've got an inventory of questions building up. Now, however, for our next panelist.

Bill Knox is again what might be called a marginal man in the highest sense of that term. As you can see, we have quite a collection of people up here. One of our panel members started as an accountant, one as a philosopher. Bill here started as a chemist. He attended Mercer University and VPI, and from 1938 to 1964 he worked for Esso Research and Engineering Company, where he progressed from research chemist to manager of the technical information division to manager of corporate planning. He left Esso in 1964 and joined the staff of the Office of Science and Technology in the executive offices of the President of the United States, where he assumed charge of stimulating the development of more effective scientific and technical information systems. His responsibilities also included the broad question of how one manages a research effort.

In late 1966 Mr. Knox joined McGraw-Hill, where he is now vice president. He is responsible there for advising and assisting management in advancing McGraw-Hill's interest in information systems

and services. Mr. Knox has been a consultant on technical information management to numerous government agencies, including—still
—the Office of Science and Technology. He holds numerous patents
and is the author of several articles on information research and
management.

II. Presentation by Mr. Knox

The essence of what I shall have to say about the role of
the manager with respect to information systems in the year 2000
might be best expressed by this little parody on Joyce Kilmer's
"Trees":

> I think that I shall never see
> A computer made like me.
>
> A me who likes martinis dry
> And on the rocks a little rye;
>
> A me who looks at girls and such,
> But mostly girls, and very much;
>
> A me who wears an overcoat
> And likes a risqué anecdote;
>
> A me who taps his foot and grins
> Whenever dixieland begins.
>
> They make computers for a fee,
> But only moms can make a me.

And this will still be true in the year 2000!

More seriously, the impact of the new information technology on
our civilization has only recently begun to dawn on me in more than
an elementary fashion. I have stumbled on it slowly, and now I am
somewhat overwhelmed with the awesome prospects ahead of us.

Wes says we have a long way to go yet. I agree, but I am concerned that we examine the alternative scenarios along the direction we wish to travel rather carefully because, as is the case with all technologies, we have before us now the choice between using our increased knowledge for good or for evil. I believe frankly that we are faced, in exploiting the new information technologies, with the same kinds of questions that faced the nations of the world—ours along with the rest—when we discovered how to make H-bombs. How shall we use them? Will the end be good—or bad?

Let me just say what I really mean by the new information technologies and why I think they are so significant. I believe that the pulling together of all of our devices and techniques, intellectual and physical—that is, the computer, the satellite, microphotography, CRT and remote access displays, input-output devices, and all the other hardware that goes with the communication of information, plus the software, the programming, and the other informational substantive content—constitutes the biggest technological revolution mankind has experienced since the invention of language itself. That's a pretty formidable statement. As I said, I haven't come to it easily or quickly; it has been borne in on me only as I learned more about the potential impact of our awesome and decidedly expensive information systems.

One of the public-policy issues that we have to face is to make sure these technologies are the servants, not the masters, of the people. In the early stages of computer-based information systems, a few systems created for military command and control ended up trying to force people to act in uniform, predictable ways. In the end the systems were modified because people wanted to be in control of the system and not have the system control them.

I think it is important for managers to discuss, debate, and ultimately reach some tentative decisions about the matter of user-orientation of information systems, and the matter of the user's (the human individual's) power to reward or penalize the developers of information systems employing all these new technologies. How can we—when the systems cost so much—actually make them responsive to what you and I want, and not to what some systems designer, systems manager, or management planner thinks we should have?

The exploitation of the new information technologies—or, let's say, part of them—is open for us to observe in the case of commercial TV and radio. These were both very important innovations; they involve, of course, the transmission of information by wireless and the use of cathode-ray tubes for transmission of pictures as well as sound. Now, they actually serve individuals, I think, in a rather rudimentary fashion. The individual has generally an on/off choice. He selects from a rather limited information or substantive base; he has a limited number of channels, in other words. He cannot get from the medium what he really wants most; he has to take what it is willing to give him at that point in time. The decision that he makes, on or off, has almost no effect on the system itself; the system goes on broadcasting even when he turns the set off. His action may change the program content slightly over the long pull, but it doesn't change the system's capability to respond when he turns it on. It's frozen, more or less, in terms of hardware.

Yet I believe that the new technologies offer us for the first time since we began to build these new information systems—telephone, telegraph, phonograph, radio, TV, advanced photographic processes, and so on—the technical potentiality for grouping them together and making them (as a system) the servant of individual people. Not as the mass audience we now are, receiving what the system gives us, but instead having in our individual environments an information console or other connection with the total information system so that we can get out of it what we want and only what we want.

It isn't going to be easy, and I certainly don't see at this point how we will do it. I simply say that managers are going to be faced with this problem. We as individual human beings will be faced with it, and I think that the manager of the year 2000 will still be wrestling with the puzzle.

Those managers will also have another problem, and I now speak as the father of children who have entered the productive age group themselves. I refer, in other words, to the gap between the generations. The manager of the year 2000 is going to need a greatly enlarged ability to appreciate, to encourage, and to utilize the people who will have grown up over the past 20 or 30 years—that is, from 1970 on. This is the group that will have had access during its entire lifetime to these new technologies.

I am reminded of what Dr. Gilbreth said this morning in her assessment of the wonderful potentialities now open to children. We theorize that stimulation of the brain actually is responsible for the development of those rather intricate convolutions in the cerebral cortex that we suppose connote our level of intelligence. The more convolutions, the higher the degree of intelligence. Research on animals has shown that the withholding of stimulation during early life results in a rather smooth cortex, whereas stimulating it results in many more convolutions. In other words, there is partial confirmation of our theory. We know, too, that human infants deprived of stimulation during their early years develop a mental set which may be related to the absence of cerebral convolutions—a mental set which makes them incapable of operating at what would have been their potential capability.

I can see children beginning at age two, or perhaps even earlier, to fool with the typewriter as an input device, operating a slide display in the nursery, developing a fantastic intellectual capability far beyond that—on the average—of the managers then in positions of authority. I wonder if management will be willing to appreciate, encourage, and utilize the talent of these children. It's a problem. Already we have many institutions in our society where creative thinking and innovation are not particularly encouraged. This is the so-called organizational syndrome. And the differences in human capabilities are not nearly so sharp today as the differences I can see coming down the road. That is why I pose this as a very real problem for management in the year 2000.

Finally, one last policy issue that I would like to raise is the structure of our society under the impact of the new technologies. I'll address myself here simply to the people who traditionally handle information—universities, publishers, government agencies, professional societies, trade associations, and so on—and who are in the business of collecting, processing, and distributing it. Will the new technologies make any difference in their respective roles? They already have certain responsibilities with the Gutenberg technology, the printed word, but I predict that there will be a shift as the new technologies take hold. I don't know what their proper roles should be. I can suggest, for example, that the government's proper role (the Federal Government's, that is) should be simply to acquire information in the raw state and make sure that there are information banks available; to leave it up to the people more closely attuned to the marketplace to take that information and then prepare packages of it for retailing to the individual user.

I can see the same thing happening to professional societies. Up until now they have played a very important role in science, technology, and certain other areas in that they have actually been retail marketers of information. However, the job is getting beyond their capabilities as the new technologies become more prevalent.

From what little I know about the publishing industry (with its rather intimate knowledge of the marketplace and the needs of the individual user), I would say that it too is moving, although probably much more slowly than it should, to exploit these new technologies. As to our universities, they have of course had a very interesting and important role in the development of books and other informational devices. They are probably the primary place where books originate, although the university presses have never accounted for a high percentage of our total book output. But with computers on university campuses, and the information already there, the temptation will be strong to expand informational programs so that the universities may in fact become a much more important force in the development of retail information packages for marketing to the individual user.

These, in summary, are the three main issues that I believe we are going to have to face: (1) The new technologies must be made to serve the people. (2) Managers must learn to appreciate, encourage, and utilize the young men and women who have grown up with the new technologies. And (3) these new technologies inevitably will have an impact on the structure of our society.

MR. BOETTINGER: When I mentioned our attempt to triangulate the truth here, I didn't realize we would be taking such long shots, as the civil engineers have it. And now we are ready for our third fix.

My rhetorical skills just can't do justice to Norman J. Ream's biography. He started life as an accountant at the university of Illinois, later working with the Pure Oil Company, IBM, and Lever Brothers—it sounds as though he'd almost made a sightseeing tour through the industrial guide. In 1953 he settled down with Lockheed, where he spent about 12 years, ending as director of systems planning.

In 1965 Norm was selected to be director of the Center for Computer Sciences and Technology in the National Bureau of Standards, U.S. Department of Commerce—the first position of its kind established in the government. He stayed there until November 1966, when he was appointed by the Secretary of the Navy to the post he now holds —that is, Special Assistant to the Secretary of the Navy.

III. Presentation by Mr. Ream

One approaches an occasion such as the dedication of the Manager Learning Center of The American Foundation for Management Research not only with a sense of great privilege but with one of humility as well. For the Foundation has assumed a very ambitious and critical role in molding the future world of management in our country.

Less ambitious is the attempt I am about to make at characterizing what that future might look like. I step very cautiously to the podium in this regard because of the tremendous uncertainty which one has to associate these days with any period much beyond the immediate or very near future. And, not being a scientist, I realize that I cannot be helpful by revealing to you any new scientific or technological breakthrough. Yet we all know that what the year 2000 will look like is very highly dependent upon the scientific discoveries and resulting technological applications which will occur between now and then.

As one who has used both proven and experimental management techniques and who, at least from my vantage point, has always attempted to push the state of the art, I hope that I may make some contribution toward a better understanding of the world ahead.

I realize that the paths taken in basic scientific research and discovery are not usually directed by the needs of the industrial environment. I do believe, and I think you will agree, that the directions of the technologies which *emerge* from basic research and development are very much charted by recognition of the needs of industry. The courses taken are usually those selected by the true navigators of the industrial community—those who understand the areas of commerce where there is waning effectiveness and where there is potential technological contribution. In saying this I am suggesting that there is more for management than a return on investments made in technology. There is responsibility as well—earned or unearned, acknowledged or not acknowledged. This responsibility implies a willingness on our part to use the new people and tools to the best advantage and to influence their development toward the desirable goals of free enterprise.

This is an important point, I believe, because until recently managers have not picked up this gauntlet, and all too many still do not. In fact, the general public has demonstrated a great deal more flexibility and willingness to accept change than has the world of management. This is not difficult to understand, for there has been in the past a high degree of success in business through the use of staid principles and self-developed, highly individualized, stylistic approaches to management. It is in this kind of world that we saw the emergence of the great business tycoons. But that was another time, when it was possible to think of an idea, produce a salable item, sell the product, and nearly monopolize the market for an extended period. Products and marketing channels were reasonably easy to develop and could be had in a short span of time.

Today the marketplace has changed. The public is much more demanding. The level of our standard of living has risen, which in turn has contributed to the complexities of management. The lead time for the research, design, and development of new product lines has lengthened, yet the life cycle of the product has been shortened. The risks associated with market innovations are much higher, but the profit rate is much lower. The capital investments are higher, and the cost of risk capital is much higher. Talent, in both the management and the scientific arenas, is much more transient among competing organizations, and the knowledge required to manage the complex organizations in today's business environment is so great that it requires strong functionalization in management, with all the pitfalls thereof. One only has to look at today's organizational structure in a representative company to recognize that the president can no longer personally know everything he has to know to conduct company operations in this highly competitive business environment. In other words, gentlemen, the name of the game has changed.

It is not difficult to find managers who nod approval of advanced management theories and practices that have been fostered by our changing environment. However, it is very difficult to find managers who not only approve of these theories and practices but employ them in the management of their concerns.

I would like to approach my subject matter by first reviewing the growth of knowledge that has taken place in our growing society since World War II. I would then like to point to some of the scientific, academic, industrial, governmental, and sociological implications that result from this growth of knowledge and to problems which we may anticipate in the decades between now and the end of this century. I would like to touch on these various areas because, in my opinion, they are interrelated.

THE GROWTH OF KNOWLEDGE

If we look at the rate of the growth of knowledge—or, for that matter, that of any other growth area—it seems that the experience of recent years has been away from things happening at a uniform or linear rate and toward things occurring exponentially and in more complicated nonlinear ways. (Perhaps this accounts for our growing interest in nonlinear programming just about the time when we have learned to use linear programming to some advantage. It isn't that it is so difficult to prepare or solve multiple equations, especially with the aid of computers, but it is getting more and more difficult to fit the real world into these equations.)

I believe it is true that many rates of growth in widely diverse fields have changed exponentially in recent years. A glance at a few of them might be both instructive and enlightening in looking toward the future.

Knowledge in the physical sciences is said to be doubling every 15 years, while growth in the social and management sciences is doubling every 50 years.[1] This may explain why we are less adept in handling the social or "people" problems which do not have a numerical or logical basis. These are the kinds of problems which not only take up the larger portion of the manager's time and energies but which, in fact, are behind most of the fundamental issues of the day. Yet we know that the physical sciences have been playing increasingly important roles in the social science areas. This infusion and cross-breeding of ideas is certain to further increase the rate at which knowledge is gained in the social sciences, so that by the year

[1] Ellis A. Johnson, "Crisis in Science and Technology," *Operations Research*, Vol. 6, No. 1, 1958, pp. 11–34.

2000 we may see the beginnings of some crucial advances in the world of nonquantum, nonlogical heuristic activity.

It is a *challenge* to the most imaginative mind to consider the body of knowledge that will exist in this country in the year 2000, even at current growth rates. It is *overwhelming* to consider further that this growth rate will be, not constant (as it has not been since about 1700 A.D.), but logarithmic. To attempt to make sense out of it all in terms of what we must do today to prepare for that world is at best *bewildering*.

Impact on Science. The expansion of scientific knowledge is relatively new. Over 90 percent of all existing technological knowledge has been assembled in the past three decades. Today we are attempting to look only 30 years ahead, and we should recognize that this problem will be severely compounded for management in the next three decades, or by the year 2000. Similarly, more than 90 percent of the world's recognized scientists are alive and active today, and their numbers also are growing exponentially.

The implications of this technological explosion are problematical at best. On the one hand we have seen a fractionation of science into highly specialized disciplines. On the other hand we see a breaking down of disciplinary boundaries. While more people have a greater depth of knowledge of a very specialized field, they are more and more required to communicate with other specialists and borrow from their disciplines. The further these boundaries break down, the more critical becomes the scientific and technical communication problem. The rate of growth of scientific journals is also exponential—from 10,000 in 1900, to some 100,000 now, to an estimated million by the end of the century. But is this a realistic direction to take? Will we see this type of medium survive as a communication vehicle by 2000 A.D.? If so, how will we manage it? If not, what will replace it as this problem burgeons?

Impact on Education. The changes we have seen taking place in the scientific world have inevitably found their way back to the university campus. In 1940 there were a million and a half degree-credited students enrolled in American institutions of higher education. Last fall there were nearly four times as many. Advance data I have received from the Office of Education's National Center for Educational Statistics show that half again as many, or over 9 million, students will be enrolled in 1976.

Only a part of the increase is due to the population growth. Other factors are very significant, I believe, and the growth and improved accessibility of knowledge play a leading role.

It is also worthy of note that the product of these enrollments has changed. The same sources show that in 1940 bachelor's degrees constituted 86 percent and master's degrees 12 percent of all degrees awarded. Projected 1976 figures show that, although there will be nearly five times as many bachelor's degrees awarded in 1976 as there were in the summer of 1940, the proportion of those degrees to the total will be some 10 percent *less!* There will be a corresponding increase in the proportion of master's degrees awarded. Doctor's degrees will remain at a relatively constant 3 percent of all degrees awarded.

These statistics show a seemingly dramatic increase in the level of education of our sources of national leadership. What they do not show is the changing meaning of that education.

In 1947 MIT graduated civil engineers, mechanical engineers, electrical engineers, and some individuals designated simply as engineers. This year MIT graduated students with the same degrees but with different end products. The civil engineer had only a remembrance of the surveying course of 20 years ago, yet he had a respectable working knowledge of automatic data processing. He was also more adept in the humanities. There were more of the unspecified engineering degrees awarded, not because there were more people who couldn't make up their minds, but because of the changed curriculum. For it is under the seemingly generalized heading of "engineer" that so many highly specialized hybrid educations have been achieved. Specifically, I refer to such specialities as aeronautics and astronautics; biochemical engineering; economics and engineering; and humanities and engineering—to mention a few. While the departmental names appear much the same to the late-middle-aged alumnus, the internal structure of departmental curricula has undergone a metamorphosis. Politics, computer sciences, simulation, and economics have entered the course vocabularies.

Of more significance, perhaps, than the statistics I have mentioned with regard to the growth rate of enrollments in institutions of higher learning is another trend which is being watched by analysts of the National Center for Educational Statistics. That is the growing trend toward the establishment of educational extension centers. Purdue, for example, has some 9,000 students enrolled in off-campus centers. Again this is a reflection of the improving accessibility of information.

Whereas, years ago, the alternative to attending classes at a college or university campus was to take a correspondence course, now the same course is often available at a nearby extension center, but with the added value of the teacher-student relationship and the classroom environment which heretofore was available only to the person who lived in or near a college town.

I suspect that widespread use of such centers also began shortly after World War II when these centers began to spring up on military bases overseas. American International College's extension centers in Bermuda and Saudi Arabia were early examples. Today this trend is considerably more apparent. When I leave the Pentagon evenings, it seems as though I am rewalking the corridors of Illini Union Hall at Illinois. It is a veritable honeycomb of classrooms for the University of Maryland, American University, and George Washington University. I know that the same thing is going on in the Department of Agriculture and other U.S. Government agencies. Similarly, I have heard of the same kind of arrangements being made for the teaching of special courses in business organizations.

At the same time that we see the increasing use of extension centers, we observe that the larger universities are getting even larger. More people are attracted to institutions with enrollments in the area of 30,000 to 40,000 students.

We will return to these points later as we look to the problems which we may expect to face around 2000 A.D. Meanwhile, we see that our national leadership sources from which we draw our "chiefs," if you will, are improving greatly—both in number and in quality—and will undoubtedly continue to improve throughout the century.

Other interesting things are happening in our educational world. Information available from the National Center for Educational Statistics also reveals that the estimated percentage of students who will be in two-year programs in 1976 is approximately 20 percent of all students who will be enrolled in institutions of higher learning at that time. This is double the same proportion for 1940. More people who in the past would have stopped at the high school level will continue their educations. By the same token, the bachelor's degree will be within the reach of more such individuals. This will have significance, as we will see later, for the managers who hire these people.

As with the degree institutions, the content of these two-year programs is changing. We are seeing a shift away from the traditional cookbook, how-to-do, "trade school," or "vocational" orientation of the junior colleges and toward theory, principles, and fundamental disciplines. Studies financed by the Carnegie Corporation and Ford Foundation have borne out this changing approach as being the only realistic way in which to prepare individuals for the modern business world.[2]

The "chiefs," then, are not the only individuals commanding our attention. We also see the burgeoning of a relatively expensive and highly trained technical workforce in greater numbers and improved quality.

Impact on Industry. What has been the impact of this knowledge explosion on industry? I believe that some of the answers can be found in what John Kenneth Galbraith calls the consequences of modern technology,[3] each one of which is the logical predecessor of the next. As I understand them, they are as follows:

1. Production costs more.
2. Tasks take longer to complete.
3. Greater investments of time and money require greater commitment to and inflexibility of plans.
4. Technology requires specialized manpower.
5. Specialization requires organization.
6. Precise planning is essential.

We have seen signs of these things for years. But we cannot afford to disregard them now. By the end of the century those who did ignore them will not have survived in this country as paying businesses or effective government organizations.

There can be no doubt that what is happening in science and education is also happening in industry, and for many of the same reasons. As more usable knowledge becomes available to managers, they have to find new ways to cope with it and employ it effectively. We have seen strong evidences of this already. It wasn't very long ago when our universities were teaching management for the sake of

[2] Hilliard R. Griffen, "Manpower—Accounting's Acute Problem," *The CPA,* July–August 1967, AICPA, Inc., New York, p. 2.
[3] John Kenneth Galbraith, *The New Industrial State,* Houghton Mifflin Co., Boston, 1967, p. 13.

management. A student educated in the principles of management, we were told, could manage anything from a dry cleaning establishment to a hospital to an automobile plant. Today a young man applying for a position cannot simply say that he is interested in a management position. A skilled personnel interviewer, who is himself a product of specialization, will ask, "What special knowledge or skills do you intend to contribute to this organization? Do you have training in textiles? Are you a biologist by education? What do you know about advancements in the area of cybernetics and how they may be applied to *our* production management problems?"

Similarly, the leaders in modern industry find it increasingly difficult to communicate with the younger specialists. More of them are needed in more fields—if the organization is to take advantage of the information which is there for the asking. The manager who does not understand the languages these men speak will neither trust what he is told nor use the new knowledge in his decision-making process and have it reflected in his organization. If he does not use this new capability, then, of course, the good specialist will abandon him for greener pastures. It is not difficult for a man to find another job these days. Specialization is a fact of modern business life which must be acknowledged and used to its greatest advantage in growing organizations.

Modern industry must make use, not only of the increasing wealth of scientific and technological knowledge, but of the tools which have sprung from that knowledge. The computer has reached into nearly every sector of today's industrial complex. In the automobile industry we see automation and cybernetics playing increasingly important roles in the design and production processes. The same is true in the steel industry—and should be, but is not, in the shipbuilding area. Our reluctance to retool our thinking is mainly due to the commitment of managers to the old ways and to obsolescent value systems. In other states where industrialization is new, such as Japan, this commitment to the past is not a deciding factor, and we are seeing steel and shipbuilding industries emerge which are more modern in methods than our own. We cannot afford to think that, because we were the first highly industrialized nation, we will automatically remain superior. This will not happen simply in deference to our age as an industrial power. Science and technology provide us the wherewithal to do what we must. It is essentially a matter of choosing to gear up our organizations with the necessary objectives, people, and tools to use what we have available to us.

In addition to the impact of knowledge on the traditional industries, we have seen and will continue to see the emergence of whole new industries, such as those in the aerospace and computer fields. In postwar America, 80 percent of our aircraft industry was blue collar and 20 percent white collar. Today it is reversed to a 40:60 relationship; and the makeup of that 60 percent has changed drastically from the earlier 20 percent, which was nearly all from engineering resources. It is now an admixture of engineers, physical and social scientists, and systems people.

Impact on Government and Warfare. The growth of knowledge has had a tremendous impact on the government as a whole, an area that could provide subject matter for a week of seminars. However, I am sure you are all aware of the growing complexity of the Federal Government—and, for that matter, of state and local governments. This is evidenced by the creation of new departments and the realignment of older ones.

Time permits me to discuss only a portion of the government problem today, but I have chosen what I consider to be two very representative problem areas in government: those of weapon systems selection and personnel specialization. (I might add parenthetically here that these difficulties are very consistent with those experienced in other sectors of our national life.)

The lifetime of weapon systems has decreased so sharply over the past 500 years that one dares not mathematically work out the lifetime of such systems in the year 2000 and beyond. Around 1000 A.D. weapons had a lifetime of about 400 years. Today that lifetime is in the area of five years, making systems obsolescent by first production. And, as the useful life of such systems decreases, one views the explosive increase in time and investment associated with their development into operational systems with similar awe. Ellis Johnson suggests that this trend is closely associated with the growth of knowledge, which permits more and more combinations and permutations—more choices.[4] Norman Precoda has told us that there were four major parameters available to an aircraft designer in 1935—propulsion, payload, speed, and defensive armament (guns or no

4 Ellis A. Johnson, *op. cit.,* p. 14.

guns) .[5] He showed how each of those parameters opened up several alternatives for the designer of 1955, so that in all he had over 360 possible choices.

If one includes parameters which were not included by Precoda, such as basing (land-based, water-based, or carrier-based) or control (piloted and pilotless), one can see that even in 1955 the choices were considerably broader. If we add the configuration choices available in 1967 (fixed-wing, variable-wing, VTOL, helo) and the newer payloads feasible in modern warfare, it can be seen that today's designer faces upward of 17,000 choices. This is true even if we recognize that some choices are not very likely choices at all, such as piloted subsonic aircraft with thermonuclear payloads, and others that are scientifically unsound (for example, supersonic, turboprop aircraft).

It may be expected that in 2000 A.D. we will be able to add sufficiently to the lists of possibilities within the stated parameters and within new parameters to at least quadruple the number of choices currently available. And, if you agree that these kinds of choices are staggering to the aircraft designer, consider the defense manager, who must weigh these choices against all other possible weapon systems—missiles, ships, and tanks, for example.

Thus it is clear that the choices which will be open in all endeavors in 2000 stagger the imagination of our most liberal associates. It can also be seen that great costs are presently associated with the making of choices, whether it be in government or industry. A recent example of this was the decision to bring a battleship out of mothballs for the Vietnam conflict: The cost of refitting the battleship is estimated at $24.8 million. The cost of the study which was made to support the decision itself was $750,000. Moreover, still greater costs will be required to make choices in the future, primarily as a result of the increasing number of choices available. As these costs and associated risk levels rise, so will decision levels, and necessarily so.

In all this we are talking about making what we call the "best" choice. As the numbers of possible choices rise exponentially with the growth of knowledge, it may become necessary to use other values. It may be more effective and economical for a product manager to choose a product which satisfies his requirements rather than

[5] Norman Precoda, "Air Weapon Systems Analysis," *Operations Research,* Vol. 4, 1956, p. 6888.

one which optimizes them, particularly if it can be made in larger numbers and with greater speed than his competitor's optimized, but obsolescent, product.

There can be no doubt that traditional professional lines have also broken down throughout our military society. If I may favor the Navy momentarily, I can illustrate. Twenty years ago the naval officer corps consisted mainly of two kinds of officers, surface officers and aviation officers, supported by a few smaller corps of staff specialists in such areas as supply and medicine. These were the "disciplines," if you will, of our officer corps, since the kind of education or degree held by an officer was not regarded as critical at that time. Now these professional disciplines have greatly increased in number (in the 1947, or postwar, Navy there were none—today there are 74), and each has a number associated with it. This number is termed a "designator." Designators are attached to billet descriptions, and until recently it was largely on the basis of designators that staff assignments were made.

However, an officer may now also be assigned another number which is called a "P-Code" or "S-Code" and which identifies his postgraduate degree, or otherwise gained subspecialty, as well as any other academic or functional specialty such as operations research, financial management, and so on. Today there are 84 different P- and S-Codes recognized by the Navy. Interestingly enough, the tendency is away from the use of designators for purposes of assigning particular officers to particular staff billets, except where shipboard or aviation skills are obviously required, and toward assignment by P- and S-Codes. In fact, the number of designators has decreased since 1952. Similarly, the Navy has established skill codes for its enlisted ranks. In the past ten years the number of these codes has increased from some 360 to 576.

It can be readily seen that these developments are representative not only of all our military departments but of government in general.

Impact on Society. Let us now turn to a more general view of the growth of knowledge and its impact on our society as a whole. One of the most significant effects that technology has had on society has been in the changing pattern of the workforce. Look at the articles in our major newspapers relating to unemployment, which is in the area of 5 percent. Then turn to the back pages of those papers and read the classified advertisements. You will see columns full of employment opportunities in technical skill areas. The changing structure of our economy has had the effect of reducing drastically the number of noncreative jobs on the labor market. While our labor force still reflects the old requirements for manpower, our requirements for technical skills have escalated beyond our ability to satisfy them.

This imbalance in the labor force, with its attendant fostering of unemployment, cannot in itself be blamed for the social unrest which exists in our country today. However, it certainly has intensified the critical issues of the day, which have found their way to the streets of Detroit, Milwaukee, and Newark, to mention a few.

Even religion is undergoing its most severe change since the Reformation. The ecumenical movement has brought together the leaders of the different Christian sects, for the first time in four centuries, to talk about problems confronting Christianity in the 20th century. Such a movement, however, is not without its pain to church leaders; for it fosters an environment in which members of the clergy vocalize about many of the problems of the day. Whereas in the past the clergy provided a quieting influence in our society, today religious leaders of many denominations are the harbingers of social action. Maybe this is the catalyst, and the adhesive, that could lead to true ecumenicalism and spiritual unity.

One of society's most pressing problems is the teacher shortage which has plagued us since World War II and the GI Bill. Many of you have, I suspect, received some training under this program. Nonetheless, the teacher supply/demand imbalance is still with us, and it grows in intensity with the growth of knowledge. As new specialties are created to answer the demands of government and industry, a new demand is placed for the same individuals in the teacher force. The problem of meeting these demands is heightened by the fact that supplies of scarce talent are quickly usurped by high-paying industries. The result, of course, is that the creators of the supply—the specialized teachers—are depleted so rapidly that the supply cannot begin to match the demand.

As I look about today, I see radical changes taking place in the family unit. Our thirst for knowledge and the self-inflicted demands on our leisure time seem almost to be destroying family unity. With night courses, Little League baseball, dancing schools, P-TA meetings—all the results of a demanding society—when do parents have the time to implant in children the real essence and meaning of life? And shouldn't our great technical cybernetic know-how be addressed also to matters of convenience, such as helping the housewife in her daily responsibilities—getting the laundry from the bedrooms to the washer and dryer and back, for example? Trivial? How many things can you think of which are as important as freeing a mother to permit her more time with her children? Not many, I suspect. Yet each year we see rising statistical evidence of juvenile crime, divorce, and widespread personal unhappiness in our affluent society. We hear talk about sending our children to school at an earlier age. What of the critical and very brief time a mother has to instill a sense of values in her children before they are thrust into production-line living? Can we give our parents another hour in the day for their families?

Yet, as I speak, I know that what we do or do not do will have a long-range effect on the basic nature of our society, on the education of our daughters and the earning power of our sons, on the personal privacy of our children, on the laws and government of our nation, and on the social and cultural development of the world.

The Total Impact. We have talked briefly about the scientific, academic, industrial, governmental, and social worlds in which we live. As with everything else, we tend to build false barriers and imaginary boundaries to suit our own interests. And it is convenient for me to discuss these worlds as separate entities, even though I know better. For none of these things is happening *in vacuo.* Each has an impact on and is interlaced with the others. The problems we face must be solved, *jointly,* not alone by scientists, managers, politicians, or anyone else. Yet, even when we admit this fact, we give it only lip service. It sounds too much like a platitude. But it is not.

How many mathematicians are gathered in this room today? How many engineers? How many systems analysts? Programmers? Salesmen? How many business managers? Government policy-making officials? Educators? How many priests? Students? Patent attorneys? Constitutional lawyers? Physicians? Congressmen? Motion picture and television producers? How many judges are here? How many nurses? How many elementary school teachers? Copyright experts? How many curious laymen? How many librarians are there? How many linguists? How many government, foundation, or corporate research and development managers who control the allocation of vital resources? How many planners? How many generals and admirals?

It is unfortunate, when we gather at times such as this, that we do not see the problems we face in their true context. This is a fault of which we, as managers with supposedly wide scopes of vision, should never be guilty.

MEETING THE CHALLENGE OF CURRENT PROBLEMS .

We have talked about the tremendous changes taking place in our country and of some of the problems which these changes present. Let us now look briefly at some of the more significant efforts we have made and are continuing to make in addressing these problems.

To illustrate, in the past decade we have taken great strides in harnessing this country's scientific and technological know-how toward the achievement of national goals.[6] To begin to do this has required a great joining of hands among government agencies, academic institutions, and the private sectors of the economy.

These achievements were in large part heralded by the establishment of the post of Special Assistant to the President for Science and Technology immediately following the drama of the first successful orbiting of Sputnik in 1957. President Eisenhower appointed Dr. James R. Killian as the first Special Assistant; and the post, whose incumbent is better known as "The President's Science Advisor," is now occupied by Dr. Donald F. Hornig.

A series of important events followed that first appointment, including the establishment of the President's Science Advisory Committee (or PSAC, as it is called), which has been chaired by the Science Advisor. In essence, PSAC brought the cream of the academic and industrial science world to the White House doorstep.

Almost overnight the first recommendations of PSAC were adopted with the chartering of the Federal Council for Science and Technology by executive order on March 13, 1959. FCST comprised the top research and development policy officials from all federal

6 R. E. Barry, "Committee on Scientific and Technical Information Coordinates Interagency Information Systems," *Navy Management Review*, Vol. XII, No. 4, April 1967, pp. 3-14.

agencies involved in substantial R&D efforts. It too has been directed by the President's Science Advisor. FCST provided the framework for a viable information network among government agencies and the wherewithal to provide more effective national administration and utilization of the scientific and technological resources and facilities of federal agencies, including the elimination of unnecessary duplication. FCST committees were formed in broad program areas, and membership was derived from agencies with a major mutual interest.

To give but one example, let us consider how many government agencies have more than a passing interest in the atmospheric sciences. The Department of Agriculture is concerned with forest fire prevention, excessive watershed runoff, and effective use of pesticides. AEC is interested in fallout measurement and prediction; HEW in air pollution; the Department of Interior in water conservation; NASA in high-altitude atmospherics; the Department of Commerce in the propagation of electromagnetic waves, weather problems, and ocean commerce. The Department of Transportation is concerned with atmospheric influences on aviation and highway development and safety. The National Science Foundation has vested interests in basic aspects of meteorology and weather modification, and the Department of Defense in numerous aspects of ballistics, naval operations, air and surface warfare, and intelligence. The quasi-official National Academy of Sciences–National Academy of Engineering in its current *Highway Research in Progress* [7] lists over 200 projects in highway drainage and development which relate to the atmospheric sciences. And we could go on.

It is not difficult to imagine the tremendous communication problems surrounding such a subject area and the possibility that exists for undesired duplication of effort, expenditure of monies, and expenditure of other scarce resources. To meet the needs presented by this growing problem, FCST established as early as 1959 the Interdepartmental Committee for Atmospheric Sciences. It was through the effort of this group that the national atmospheric research effort was surveyed and evaluated and responsibilities of federal agencies were allocated.

Similarly, the Committee on Scientific and Technical Informa-

[7] *Highway Research in Progress,* Developmental Issue, Part I (of three), April 1967, Subject Areas 11–35.

tion—COSATI—was organized under the Council in 1962 because nearly all major federal agencies had become deeply involved in the use of information sciences technology. Technical libraries, document-handling systems, and information systems (including command, management and intelligence systems) have been widely employed throughout government. While these systems are primarily supported by microform and computer technologies, they draw from all portions of the information sciences.

It is my understanding that a survey just completed by the COSATI Panel on Information Sciences Technology reveals that in fiscal year 1967 there were over 2500 on-going research projects in approximately 20 different federal agencies. This survey may be published in the fall.

As a result of the work of COSATI, strides are being made toward the achievement of federal standards in such areas as microfiche specifications, technical report format, scientific and technical subject area classification, descriptive cataloguing, and guidelines for domestic and international exchange of machine-readable indexes. COSATI, the Bureau of the Budget, the Departments of Commerce and Defense, and others are actively engaged in data element standardization programs. Each of these developments will permit greater availability and exchange of information among government agencies and with industry.

Many COSATI efforts are still skeletal in development. For example, the *COSATI Subject Category List* [8] is at best an incomplete thesaurus of scientific and technical uniterms. The significant thing, however, is that it does provide the looseleaf framework from which a greater capability can be developed. I expect this and other similar capabilities to be expanded greatly with the introduction of more automated information systems and interconnecting links throughout government, educational institutions, and industry. I plead with you, gentlemen, to examine these efforts being undertaken in government and to cooperate in their advancement and take advantage of their potentials.

In addition to these programs in and among government agencies, several services have been established to facilitate the handling and exchange of information within government and between gov-

[8] *COSATI Subject Category List* (Ad 612 200), to be published in 1968 by the Clearing house for Federal Scientific and Technical Information, Springfield, Virginia.

ernment and industry. A few examples may be seen in such organizations as the Science Information Exchange [9] in Washington, which maintains a data base of indexed, on-going research projects which are sponsored by federal agencies. The Department of Commerce Clearinghouse for Federal Scientific and Technical Information maintains a supply of unclassified technical reports stemming from those research projects which it sells to the general public at the unit price of three dollars.

Similar centers support the needs of several of the departments of the Federal Government, such as Defense, NASA, and AEC. Additionally, there are numerous specialized information centers with relatively narrow scopes of subject-area interest but with in-depth coverage within those areas. The Highway Research Information Service of the National Academy of Sciences–National Academy of Engineering is one example, and there are numerous others such as the U.S. Cryogenic Data Center, the National Library of Medicine, the National Clearinghouse for Mental Health Information, and the National Oceanographic Data Center.[10] Similar kinds of specialized information centers have begun to flourish in the academic and industrial sectors, as exemplified by the University of Connecticut's Institute of Cellular Biology and the E. I. du Pont de Nemours and Company's Plastics Department Information Center.

An unusual service is offered by the National Referral Center for Science and Technology, located in the Library of Congress. It does not provide information *per se* in any subject area, but it does provide a list of knowledgeable offices in special fields and subject areas. It publishes directories in these areas, such as the directory of U.S. information resources on water.[11] This document lists some 163 pages of information sources in the subject area of water resources.

Industry has also taken some first steps forward in coping with our changing environment. Improved working conditions and better employee training and education programs are examples. There is growing evidence of greater cooperation between government agencies and industry in facing such fundamental problems as water and

---

[9] Organizationally under Smithsonian Institution and funded by National Science Foundation.

[10] *Nonconventional Scientific and Technical Information Systems in Current Use*, National Science Foundation 66-24, No. 4, U.S. Government Printing Office, December 1966.

[11] *A Directory of Information Resources in the United States, Water*, September 1966, U.S. Government Printing Office, Washington, D.C.

air pollution, research reporting, reforestation, labor-management arbitration, and standards development.

Exchange of information between industry and government is improving. I mentioned the Science Information Exchange earlier. Dr. Monroe Freeman, the director of SIE, is currently experimenting with a program wherein industry and academia are being surveyed for information pertaining to the man-years of effort being allocated in the various areas of isotope development. This information will be integrated with similar data representing the government effort. While the system will not identify the efforts of any particular corporation, it will provide managers with an appreciation of the national dimensions of work in progress in this important field. This will be of particular importance to the scientist or to the government or industrial manager who is contemplating entering this field of research, and it will be available to such people on request. If the program is successful, other fields will be studied and distribution profiles will be constructed. Again, such activity is representative of the growing confidence between government and industry.

We are learning better ways of capturing energy in the form of information and keeping it for later use. In education we see intensified programs being pursued at the federal, state, and local levels of government and in private institutions. Industry is beginning to wrestle with the knowledge that there is a great training gap among the rank and file of the workforce and a stultifying education gap in the board room.

Management obsolescence is finally being recognized as something more than a voguish term. Dudley E. Brown, group vice president of finance with Lockheed, recently warned us about the widening distance between the managerial-talent requirements of industry and the supply available to meet the demand. He further warned that there is an unplanned and probably unrecognized high obsolescence rate in the managerial field.[12]

A LOOK TO THE DISTANT FUTURE

Extrapolating into the future may sound a good deal like science fiction, but I think the technical advances we have made during the

12 "Unplanned Obsolescence: The Bane of Executives," *Los Angeles Times,* July 28, 1967, Business and Finance Section, p. 12.

past decade in computer usage, design, and application give us a reasonably decent basis from which to predict what the next three decades will portend for those of us who will be around to see it unfold.

During a period of eight years, the annual rate of improvement in computers from the standpoint of performance—speed, memory, input, and output—has been 81 percent for scientific computations and 87 percent for commercial computations. This means that approximately we improve by a factor of ten (or, therefore, by two orders of magnitude) every four years, by a factor of approximately ten every eight years, and by a factor of approximately a thousand every twelve years. On the basis of this growth pattern, and of past cost factors, I think we can reasonably state that computers are going to be relatively inexpensive in comparison with those we know today. They are going to be powerful, fast, reliable, and small in size. Large memory banks for data and programs will be centralized and accessible to large numbers of users. Time sharing will be the *modus operandi* of the day. Computers will communicate with human beings in a large variety of formats, including graphics, voice input/output, and visa-phones, and, in particular, through the use of computer-aided instruction (CAI) techniques.

The computer will be the most important scientific and management tool. It will become an integral part of the laboratory experiment complex, tied directly to other laboratory equipment. Today we tax the limit of our currently available computer capacity when we attempt a simulation for weather prediction, but tomorrow such efforts will be commonplace, perhaps providing us with enough information to modify our weather.

The most significant role that the computer will play in the future will be as an aid in simulation techniques. Laboratories, classrooms, and hospitals—as we know them today—will be quite out of style. Engineers, scientists, educators, and businessmen will be able to test or design a product or theory by using simulation techniques which can assist in determining whether it is technically possible, examining its utility, and testing its marketability. The businessman will be able to simulate a series of interrelated management decisions and determine the impact of those decisions if they are actually implemented. Great care, however, must be exercised in the use of simulation techniques to insure that we deal with the human behavioral aspects of each management problem.

I have previously touched on the different disciplines existing today that were unknown ten years ago. The future portends, I feel, an even greater explosion of specialized disciplines. Our efforts in space and interplanetary travel will trigger the creation of engineers, physicists, and scientists in fields that are today totally undreamed of. For instance, the next three decades will see further exploration of the oceans of the world—both space and sea—for it is here that man will be forced to look for the mineral wealth and food to support future generations. These efforts will create yet another group of specialists.

Let us look into some of these fields and see how computers will affect the day-to-day operations of technicians. In the field of engineering design, for example, the engineer will provide the initial matrix or form, including the performance specifications of a given item, and then ask the computer to fill in what is missing. The important contribution here is the engineer's increased ability to change things in a given design while allowing the computer to estimate the effects of such changes from the standpoint of weight, performance, cost, manufacturing, sales, and distribution problems.

Even today the accumulation of medical knowledge is tremendous—and it is growing ever more rapidly. All the more reason, then, why the doctor of the future will have to rely on the computer to store all the data available to him. Human limitations will of necessity dictate the use of this new tool in diagnosing patients' ills and in determining the proper treatment.

Already, exploratory projects are showing that the computer is turning out to be an ideal device for instructing and examining students at all levels from grammar school through high school in many diverse subject-matter areas—from the most mundane repetitive tasks to the highly sophisticated new specialist disciplines. Because computer-aided instruction is going to accelerate and broaden the learning process, the time it saves will have to be used in sharpening the reasoning and judgment skills. And the use of the computer as an educational tool must not stop in the classroom. Skills must be transferred and made available at all stages of individual and professional development; they must even penetrate the offices of top management.

How will we accomplish this? I suggest that the answer lies in three developments which I pointed to earlier. The first is the growth of the extension-center concept in education; the second is the burgeoning of specialized information centers in government, industry, and academia; and the third is the improved time-sharing and CAI capabilities being afforded us by science, technology, and the computer industry. The third, gentlemen, is little more than an extension of the first and second points. CAI *must* be brought into all levels of management activity, including the very top. Just as yesterday's graduates are obsolescent today, so will today's graduates be obsolescent in tomorrow's management world. Both must introduce and use this improved way of learning; both must also make this opportunity available to the growing numbers of those in the technical workforce who will have completed two-year educational programs and who will be thirsting for the chance to continue their educational pursuits.

This is consistent with the trend toward a shorter working week. We should plan for this eventuality and provide for a correspondingly longer "education week." I can foresee the likelihood and desirability of a four-day working week and a one-day educational week. It is as plain as can be that sabbaticals will not do in our rapidly changing world. It is obvious that the scientific and professional journals will not suffice as the knowledge base expands exponentially before us. It is clear that the old-fashioned business or professional-society conference will die on the vine as an "art form" in the increasingly competitive and dynamic environment. Painful though the process may be, we must reappraise the old ways.

The rate at which specialities have proliferated in the past will continue to increase rapidly as man continues to explore in and out of his normal environment. With this increased number of skills there will be a corresponding increase in information and information-manipulation requirements that will make today's information storage, retrieval, and manipulation needs seem archaic and infinitesimal by comparison.

CONCLUSION

In closing, I would like to refer briefly to the lovely brochure which has been distributed on the occasion of this dedication. It contains a sketch of what presumably is a manager before a remote display device. The caption highlights the objectives of The American Foundation for Management Research, which may be summarized as follows:

1. To collect and make available information on existing management practices;
2. To conduct or cause to have conducted research into new management practices;
3. To foster the application of research in the management world.

May I say that managers have traditionally favored the first of these objectives—the easiest and the most comforting. For a certain sense of security may be derived from learning that everyone else is doing things the same way we think we are. It makes our position seem stronger when it is challenged. It is the latter two areas where we are the weakest and where we lack leadership in finding and using the techniques we need if we are to do the job we have asked for. AMA and the Manager Learning Center, in particular, have assumed the very responsible role of providing that leadership so that the man in the picture will be looking ahead—not behind.

I am afraid that I have used up all the time that has been allotted me to cover the tremendous breadth of this subject matter. However, I would like to state that within the next decade it will be generally understood that the prime challenge will turn, not around the production of goods and services, but around the difficulties and opportunities involved in a world of extreme change and widening choices. I would like to leave these thoughts with you:

- No product will be safe in an innovating world.
- No enterprise, however big, is safe in an era of radical change; all organizations must live dangerously and try to hear the potentialities in the marketplace.
- No management technique can survive as a conditioned response to a given situation, for the situations will not remain static.
- No business or marketing plan can avoid becoming obsolete when there are vast swings in mass habits, when there is intense and imaginative competition.
- No member of management is secure in his position unless

he can cope with extreme change. Past successes will not secure his future.

Finally, I believe the statement made by Jean Monnet, the architect of the European Common Market, is very apropos in our own given situation. "We must not be overimpressed by material problems. They are not very hard to resolve. What counts is to make up our minds to see things in the perspective of building the future, not of preserving the past." [13]

MR. BOETTINGER: Before we take a stand-in-place isometric, let me just sum up.

Wes, Bill, and Norman have done the triangulation job superbly. I recall that one of our public relations researchers said, in talking to some university teachers to get a fix on what we're going to be facing (since universities get the wave of new people first), "This is the first generation that has been brought up on TV and Dr. Spock." He attributed some of the problems we're having to cope with on campus to this phenomenon.

And another thing has impressed me this afternoon. I am struck by the sort of optimistic/pessimistic feeling that has run through all three presentations.

Other people, however, have faced similar problems, as a quotation from Plato will show. It comes from a dialogue (Phaedrus) which recounts what happened in Egypt when Thoth, who was the secretary-god and kept all the records of the dead, came down to Pharaoh and said, "This invention, O King"—he was talking about writing, of all things—"will make the Egyptians wiser and will improve their memories, for it is an elixir of memory and wisdom that I have discovered." He thought this was the greatest thing since papyrus, but the king was not convinced and feared that the invention of writing would impair the memory instead of improving it, that the people would then read without understanding. Doesn't this sound perilously close to the kind of problem we've got today?

Now for the questions. The floor is open for the first barrage.

[13] Joseph Kraft, *The Grand Design: From Common Market to Atlantic Partnership,* Harper & Bros., New York, 1962, p. 11.

Discussion

QUESTION: Mr. Knox, copyright as it now exists forms a barrier to free reduplication of information, particularly in view of the concept of a duplicating library. What future accommodation will be necessary on the part of copyright holders and republishers if freer exchange is to result?

MR. KNOX: If I knew that, a lot of the controversy that is probably scheduled for us over the next three years could be eliminated.

I'm glad you used the word "accommodation," however, because I think it is an accommodation that will be required, and actually an accommodation is in prospect already. I'm sure you are aware that Senator McClellan has proposed the setting up of a national commission to study this very question in connection with the copyright revision act. There are hopes that this will be done.

Actually, I must say there's a paucity of evidence as to whether copyright has hurt, hampered, or otherwise limited the development of new systems employing the new technologies. I haven't seen any systems whose research and development have been held back because of copyright restrictions. Again, if I may plead a large amount of ignorance and a small amount of knowledge with respect to publishers, I believe it is true that they grant copyright permission rather freely. Therefore, no one who is undertaking scholarly or educational work should have a problem at present. The problem is one for the future, and it's my hope that a satisfactory accommodation will be reached before that future becomes the present.

QUESTION: On the assumption that we are going to have a tremendous amount of data which is retrievable—and is going to be readily available to a number of people in business, science, industry, and so forth—is this going to encourage centralization or decentralization as it applies to large universities, large industrial businesses, and the like?

MR. BOETTINGER: I think this question has two parts. Wes, why don't you take the first part? Norm, you take the second.

DR. CHURCHMAN: There seem to me to be two forces operating here. One tends strongly toward centralization, and the other is leaning almost exactly in the other direction. As we develop the capability of modeling large organizations—and to some extent that capability already exists—then the old-fashioned decentralization will begin to wither away. I understand from some of my friends that there is now a linear programming model that handles 2 million variables and 35,000 equations, which is quite a lot to put on a computer. When that capability is made available, there will be a kind of centralization occurring. It's not the old-fashioned kind, and it's not decentralization, but it's much more centralization than many people will be happy with. On the other hand, time sharing is, of course, altogether feasible from a hardware point of view and soon will be feasible from the software point of view. This makes the decentralization capability greater.

Both forces, as I say, are being felt. Whether you want to link the units of an organization so that decisions are cycled through one part only or cycled through the whole entity is going to be the great debate. Logically, it seems as though we should include the entire organization, since we know that the components of a system are so inseparable that it hardly makes sense not to link them. When we do, you'll have a much stronger centralization.

MR. BOETTINGER: Norman, since your activity, by its essence, is decentralized, how are you going to resolve this problem?

MR. REAM: I can't exactly agree with Wes on this answer; I think that the problem of centralization versus decentralization, if we look at it from the standpoint of industry, is a matter of management philosophy. It depends on what management wants to do. The way industry is developing today, with the merging and diversification that are taking place, will lead us away from centralization—that is, the centralization of the management of day-to-day operations.

I would like, in short, to make a distinction between the management of day-to-day operations and management in the sense of planning for the future. I think they're quite different, and I think that the long-range planning—the effort that determines what the corporation should be like 20 or 25 years hence and what part it will play in the industrial environment—will probably be handled on a centralized basis. It almost has to be handled that way because diversification will continue. But along with this diversification we also will have the divorce procedure that has to take place as the company continues to operate. It will be dropping product lines, even dropping subsidiaries along the way, and you can hardly expect local managements to divorce themselves automatically from such decisions. They're human, and they can't be expected to cut themselves and their responsibilities from the corporate body. But the day-to-day operations that are their proper concern *will* be decentralized.

I don't think that the information available has much to do with this problem. It's a human problem involving the question of how much a small nucleus of men can control and control well. No matter how much information a person has, the amount he can digest and use rationally is bound to be limited.

MR. KNOX: Norman has said that a lot depends on what you want to achieve—the objectives of your organization. I believe that decentralization probably started because it was difficult for headquarters to have all the information in a central bank, and be able to respond in timely enough fashion at the local level to the problem that was created at that level. It's a matter of poor communication and the absence of information. Now, however, with the new hardware, we've gotten away from those limitations. Which brings us face to face with the basic question whether there are other things about the management process, other parameters, that make decentralization or centralization desirable. It's not only a question of control; there's a question of values here. I would guess that there will be operations—let's say business firms as opposed to government or university or other nonprofit organizations—where top management will want operating management to compete rather vigorously at the local level; therefore, they will still want decentralized decisions.

MR. BOETTINGER: From day to day.

MR. KNOX: Yes, even though, looked at from a systems point of view, this may be an inefficient way to do business. Most of us believe that profit is maximized by giving local management a challenge, and allowing decentralized decision making is one form of challenge. But other factors are coming into the picture daily, and management will have to think very seriously about the decentralization/centralization question.

DR. CHURCHMAN: I see nothing on the horizon that is going to do away with functionalization as we have it today. In fact, university curricula—from my point of view—are leading us toward a greater functionalization, a greater number of specialties that are branching off. This is certainly recognizable in the scientific field, but it's also very apparent in the management field. And, until that trend reverses itself, we are not going to have centralization because functionalization implies the decentralization of management. We functionalize along certain lines; we allow management at certain levels to rest so far as those functional areas are concerned; and to alter this requires a complete about-face.

We haven't addressed ourselves to the educational picture, but I would just like to say a word about it. I believe the good president of Colgate has intimated that there's going to be more and more decentralization of learning in the United States. I myself think we're going to see a four-day work week for managers plus one day of continuing education—probably with computer-assisted instruction techniques designed to keep them up to date on the various disciplines they're using within their organizations. Today we don't have the facilities, but I would suggest that in the year 2000 the manager—the professional manager—will spend at least this much time every week re-educating himself.

MR. BOETTINGER: I'd like to exercise my prerogative as chairman to ask a question of Dr. Churchman. You slipped in the idea that we might use the skills of journalists, dramatists, and so on in our model building and decision making. Furthermore, it strikes me that all we've said here involves handling a tremendous number of variables under certain constraints—which really becomes a definition of what an art is.

Wes, with your scenarios you have taken us back to Periclean Athens. What place do you see in the future for what I will call the artistic temperament which we have avoided like the plague, in so many cases, down at the recruiting office? It seems that the more I hear, the more I'm convinced that we're talking here about the quest for the esthetic man who feels his way and can handle a tremendous number of qualitative as opposed to quantitative phenomena. Do you see any place for the artistic temperament in the future?

DR. CHURCHMAN: I can tell a little story on myself that relates to the point you raise. At Berkeley we did design a scenario—it dealt with the allocation of federal funds to research and development. At that time about 90 percent of those funds went into EOD, AEC, and NASA, and the scenarios had to do with the question of whether that was a sound policy. We developed two stories about what the future, international as well as national, was going to be with respect to the utilization of R&D by the Federal Government. In order to make the briefing as balanced as possible, we put together a team of model builders, logicians, economists, and so on and built two stories—very beautiful from our point of view—which we broadcast over the educational radio station at Berkeley as an experiment.

They were incredibly dull. I said to my wife and 15-year-old son, "Listen to the radio tonight. I'm on it." Then, after we had been listening for about five minutes, my son said, "Let's turn the radio off. I can't talk while all that noise is going on." We just did not have the ability to get the reality of the future across in the dramatic way that was really essential here. We were ignoramuses in the art of telling a convincing set of stories.

We are now working with the drama department, trying to see whether we can inject into such a briefing, along with the logic, the essential drama which, as we've said, did occur in the Periclean Age and does occur in Congressional hearings now and then. Can you wed the two?

Well, it's our hope that somehow or other we can do it. Dramatists, social psychologists, and even to some extent psychoanalysts will be telling us some things that we're dreadfully ignorant about—namely, the attitudes of people while they are listening to presentations.

MR. KNOX: That's what any good publisher does.

MR. BOETTINGER: Next question.

DR. CHURCHMAN: I have a question. Both Norm and Bill have been talking about large information banks, and Bill indicates that both the two-year-old child and the 40-year-old manager will have access to these enormous facilities. I ask myself, is that desirable? Perhaps it may be altogether wrong. If it's true that the new information systems are going to be like a telephone, a natural extension of the mind, is it sound to want to have such large ones universally available? The ecology of the situation represents some real dangers. My lawyer friends tell me that, in essence, legal negotiations require you to forget a lot of the facts. If you take them all into account, then the negotiations go on forever. So I'm speculating about whether it's a question, not of having or not having large information banks, but of having good-quality information banks which aren't necessarily large.

MR. KNOX: I wouldn't take exception to that. I would just say that the information banks should be tailored to circumstances. The people who design curricula for first- and second-graders have an idea of the informational resources to which those children—on the average—should be exposed. They probably underestimate the children's capabilities, but at least they do attempt, in our public school programs, to tailor the information they provide to existing needs.

DR. CHURCHMAN: But is this being done for managers as well?

MR. KNOX: Managers have quite different needs—far-ranging, wide-ranging informational needs. I don't know exactly what form the information banks are going to take with respect to them, but I imagine the manager will build his own file as he goes along. Every time he finds some bit of information he can use, he will say, "Put this in the bank." Then, of course, he'll have to have an index reminding him that it's there. This, I think, is going to be a trial-and-error proposition where the individual manager tailors his informational resources in much the same way that he now tailors his personal library.

DR. CHURCHMAN: What about Norm's point—that he'd rather have things the manager *doesn't* want in the bank?

MR. KNOX: I don't quite buy that one. It seems to me that most people—and I'm judging by extrapolation from myself—are lazy, especially about being challenged intellectually. Relatively few people want to be told something that they don't want to believe, or something they don't want to know, or something that causes them to act differently from the way they had planned to act. They don't really like to have that kind of information; and, while it may be good from some systems point of view for them to be given it, maybe the human individual ought to remain in control of the situation. Maybe we should tolerate, in other words, people's inefficiencies and reluctance to change at whatever level. Probably people are less reluctant to change today than they were 100 years ago. Thirty years from now, they may be even less reluctant. If they are, then by all means throw in some of this information that will challenge them.

MR. BOETTINGER: I think Bill has given us an illustration of why the tenure of a director in an intelligence agency is short—because his business is not to tell anything but the bad news.

DR. CHURCHMAN: I was just going to say one thing. I think the avenues of management are strewn with the dead bodies of people who wanted to hire only people who would tell them what they wanted to hear—not what they *should* hear.

MR. KNOX: I still feel that most of our progressive and intelligent management people do want to hear adverse information, that they do want criticism. It's a matter of how it's presented to them. And I might say, Wes, as far as your large information retrieval systems are concerned, that I think they still have a long way to go in this area. We really don't know today how to store and retrieve information. We don't really know how to search for information except by old techniques.

I'm always reminded of the scientist who wanted to get all the information on venetian blinds. So, taking the key words "venetian" and "blind," he put them into the system, and got all the information on blind Venetians. This can happen; it happens all the time.

DR. BARNETT: [1] That's a permuted index.

MR. BOETTINGER: We have a question.

DR. BARNETT: I wasn't going to say anything, but there's one question for me personally in all of this discussion so far. That is, all you gentlemen are using the term "information" as though you knew what it meant. It's a very slippery word. Now, I'm a manager, and I

[1] Dr. Vincent M. Barnett, Jr., President, Colgate University. See his address on pages 34-46.

want an answer to a simple question: Who is the best contemporary American architect now practicing? This is a simple piece of information—all I want is a name so that I can get the man to design my next building. But whose judgment am I to accept? You see, the problem for me is that there is a marked distinction between information which is generally accepted—that is, information which is easily quantifiable, has a legitimacy that no one would seriously question, and is the easiest type to get—and the whole other realm of information which is the most important to managers and the most difficult to come by. This is the kind of information we have the most trouble dealing with in management.

That's a personal puzzle of my own, and I don't care who on the panel answers it.

MR. BOETTINGER: May I take it? We've got a strange juxtaposition of worlds. Dr. Barnett, the educator, gives me the hard-nosed approach, and I give a pedantic answer. It just so happens that I once tried to obtain just such a simple piece of information. It led to several hours of uproar, as a result of which I can say that your question about the architect is not an informational one.

Now, let me explain. I would separate out three things which, to me, are the essence of what we've been talking about and which we've been using interchangeably. First we have *information:* unpredictable facts, knowledge, or events which change the state or attitude of those who receive them. Information involves a flat-out yes-or-no situation; this is its nature. *Communication* is merely information which is moved from one person to another or from one place to another. But the real key to the question you asked is not information or communication but *intelligence.* And intelligence is the pattern of information which is collected for a specific purpose, and, also, the relationship of isolated pieces of information.

Your question about the architect is an intelligence question which requires the collection or communication of various pieces of information: type and purpose of building, style (Georgian or *avant garde*) , funds available, architect's fees, reputation, and availability, and so on. These many pieces of information, put together in a pattern, become the intelligence you want, tailor-made to your particular needs.

If that's too pedantic, blame my Teutonic ancestors. I still can't tell you the best architect, but if, in the words of Dr. Churchman, when you ask this question the computer can come back and say, "Not enough information; tell me more," then I think we have a dialogue that will give you the series of alternatives he spoke of. Do you want to give a young architect a chance, or do you want to play it safe? These are qualitative value judgments which can't be quantified.

DR. BARNETT: There is no such thing as the best architect.

MR. BOETTINGER: Exactly. So it's a question whose answer depends on the intelligence we furnish you, not the information we furnish you.

DR. CHURCHMAN: Excuse me. I think we are agreeing a little too fast here, Henry. You say with Dr. Barnett that we haven't been talking about information. Well, a while back we had just led up to the point that we now have the potentialities for interacting with information banks to create intelligence. If you had then said, "Yes, Dr. Barnett, all you have to do to get the name of your 'best' architect will be to sit down and tell the computer what characteristics you want in him," that would still be information. You would be told the cheapest architect you could get, the man who had the least number of jobs on hand, or whatever. But it's in the melding of those bits of information into a meaningful answer that I think your term "intelligence" comes in.

MR. BOETTINGER: To me, one of the greatest things about Mendeleyev's periodic table, at the time he invented it, was not the places he filled in but the places that he left empty. And, to some extent, the description of an empty place is a very big part of the intelligence function.

There is a gap in information here, a very serious one. Don't come back and say, "I only want hard facts," because any man who just says, "I only want hard facts," is cutting off a great source of intelligence—that is, the jigsaw-puzzle job. I don't know whether we've been responsive in the legal sense, but I hope what we've said hasn't been immaterial.

DR. BARNETT: You have accomplished my purpose, which was to emphasize that we shouldn't throw the term "information" around quite so casually.

QUESTION: At first, I was going to ask about privileged information. Now I'll ask about privileged *intelligence*.

I think that in this society we reward creativity on the part of managers, both in industry and in government, in terms of the information or intelligence that they are able to draw on in making decisions. I know from my own experience that, since the CIA problems, the universities have become very sensitive about the fact that any information they acquire immediately goes into the public domain. In a competitive field this makes it difficult to reserve for yourself information that you've acquired because you had the intelligence to get it. Now, Dr. Churchman, do you as a philosopher have any idea what's going to happen in the area of information or intelligence with respect to its being allowed to remain under the control of those who have contracted for it?

DR. CHURCHMAN: I don't have a very good idea about what's going to happen, but there's no question that the topic is being widely discussed right now. It would be unfair to say there's no awareness of the privacy issue among information retrieval people—this is something that's debated continuously. Moreover, there's Congressional interest in it.

I don't feel personally alarmed at the notion that we may at some future time find ourselves with state information systems that are disastrously accessible. The designers know of the issue, and big mistakes are not likely to be made. Just how the problem's to be solved is not clear, but it's an old issue for the new data banks—the old data banks had it too. Not everybody, after all, can get at the FBI file. What the legal situation will be in the future remains to be seen.

MR. KNOX: I think it's been said by some experts in this field that it's easier to protect privacy with the computer than it is with documents. Is this so?

MR. BOETTINGER: One of my fellows who was worrying about the privacy issue said, "My God, we're in an information explosion and I'm going to do my bit. As soon as I was born," he told me, "somebody wrote down the particulars and put them in a file. Now, whatever I eat, the supermarket data statisticians figure out just what it is. When I smoke, other people record whether it's a Camel or a Chesterfield. Just by existing and carrying on my normal activities I am contributing to the data explosion. So," he confided, "I made up my mind I was just going to sit still in a chair. And do you know what? There was an actuary with a stopwatch!"

My whole point in telling this story is that we're in a situation where, even if we stabilize the population and everyone sits still in a chair, the mere fact that people want to know more is going to produce more ways in which they find more out. The question is, will they attach these attributes to you as a statistical unit or as a specific person? I have no doubt that the statistical aggregates will be gathered in one way or another, perhaps by looking at you through a telescope and timing your actions with a stopwatch. Everywhere you move, you leave tracks of information. This has always been true. Now they are more numerous than ever, and people are paying more attention to them.

VOICE FROM AUDIENCE: Well, *I* think there's some reason for alarm. I agree that there's going to be more and more effort exerted to find out what people are doing, and I would guess it will be done in very efficient ways. What's going to be done with the information, and how ethical it is to gather such information about people, is still a philosophical issue.

DR. FARNSWORTH: [2] Will the trend toward vast information systems and data banks lead to enormous, all-encompassing industrial complexes that discourage individual enterprise?

MR. REAM: I don't know. Certainly the climate we live in today seems to favor the development of the very large organizations that you point to and, probably, the eventual extinction of the rugged individualist. Yet, if we look at the marketplace, we see that this really isn't happening. We find very small firms achieving marked success, mainly in new fields. Whereas in the older fields the laurels probably will go to the larger firms, I think that we will see a continuing and probably accelerating growth in the number of new, young organizations willing to take risks—both professionally and financially. And I don't think there'll be a great change in the pattern as it exists today.

MR. BOETTINGER: Could I add something to that? I believe that in all human affairs counterforces are set up if we move too far in any one

[2] Frank A. Farnsworth, Jr., Professor of Economics, Colgate University.

direction. So it is in the industrial or other work situation. Whatever the nature of the organization, tension or pressure is bound to exist; and, if that tension is too low, the organization's effectiveness—however measured—will not be very great. In other words, a sloppy, happy-go-lucky kind of approach may be fun for a while, but not for long. And profits, productivity, efficiency—whatever you want to call it—will suffer. And, at the opposite extreme, under a totalitarian regime tension is so high that human beings again fail to realize their fullest potential.

It is my theory that Dr. Gilbreth and her husband went into plants where tensions were high because the complexity of the work process was not understood very well; that their great contribution was to go back along this particular path and, by reducing tension on the individual, improve his efficiency. There are some who have pushed this idea too far; people have ended up doing tasks so trivial and small that they lost any sort of meaning. And then we have authorities like Herzberg and his followers saying, "Put some more enrichment in the job." This admonition also has been misunderstood. Hence the confusion. In one case it's argued that you must reduce the tension in the plant; in another, you're urged to increase the tension. Both may be correct—in different plants.

Actually, optimums occur when the tension that is created in any organization is matched to that organization. If you want an illustration, consider a high school band and the New York Philharmonic. If I put Toscanini in to conduct the high school band, the kids will be so scared that they can't even play. Now, conversely, if I put the high school band conductor in charge of the Philharmonic, the men will be bored to tears. We get optimums when we match Toscanini to the New York Philharmonic, and we get optimums when we match the high school band conductor with the high school band.

If we go far enough in the direction of the huge organization, this, I think, is going to create certain countervailing opportunities in which the little fellows are going to run between the legs of the giants—which has been the classic advantage of the small outfit. It's when they start imitating the behavior patterns of the big ones that they get in trouble. When somebody from a small organization gets a job in a big corporation, he often has difficulty. So far as data processing is concerned, we may be going to have a sort of a Hegelian

Ping-Pong match between large and small. It's a commonplace in the data processing industry that the small manufacturers go with rifle shots into the interstices between the big manufacturers and give them an awfully hard time.

This is an optimist's view of life. We've had 100,000 years of life on this planet in our present form, and we seem to have survived. Does that strike you as hopeful? Is there a pessimist in the crowd? Do you have any rebuttal to this fantasy?

VOICE FROM AUDIENCE: Well, it's a good story.

DR. FARNSWORTH: If you didn't have the little tributaries feeding it, the Mississippi would soon dry up. I think the analogy is correct. Six people get together, form a group, and fight a big corporation. Some fail; some survive—like Polaroid and Xerox. Both started small with one idea; now they're among the big boys. If this sort of thing doesn't continue, our industries will be in trouble.

MR. KNOX: I would just like to say that I believe the advances in communication and information-handling technology are going to make it possible for the larger organizations to maintain a competitive edge a little bit longer than they otherwise would. If there's anything that impresses me about a living organism such as a business firm, it's the extreme importance of communication in determining its effectiveness. It is impossible really to control an organism or an organization without communication, particularly in response to the external environment. One of the real limitations on the competitive performance of large organizations is, in fact, the inability to communicate within the organization. The new technology will give them a new lease on life for a little while.

DR. FARNSWORTH: That means they knock the Ping-Pong ball with a little more bounce. The small companies escalate the whole process.

MR. PHILLIPS: [3] I'd like to play the devil's advocate a little on this question. There's a bit of inconsistency between what you tell us is happening through the evolution of the computer and what reaction you tell us it's going to have on our environment.

For example, you talk about the amount of information or intelli-

[3] Ralph C. Phillips, Corporate Director of Purchasing, Olin Mathieson Chemical Company.

gence that can be placed into the computer, just as though all a student will have to learn in order to have the history of the universe available to him is how to use that computer. Hank Boettinger here goes back to Aristotle. He sees the student punching his little computer and getting immediate recall from Aristotle, Plato—even Stokeley Carmichael.

Now, I question how, with our ability to go to a computer and get this kind of recall—scientific data, technical data, mathematical calculations, all the tremendous variety of information a computer can provide—we can sit here and say that we're going to have all these fellows redesigning, recalculating, and relearning what can be made available to them just like that! Why redesign the Bay Bridge and the Verrazano Bridge and all the rest of them as we have been doing in the past?

And I go back to Mr. Ream, who mentioned that, as he understood it, the educational systems are still talking and teaching function. I don't see how we can claim that the computer is going to do all the things that it can do and still teach the old archaic theories of functional organization. I think that the people in the universities and colleges ought to take a good look at their situation and ask themselves just what a university or a college is. Are we still going to have students sitting eyeball to eyeball with us in a class? The answer, of course, is no; we've already been told that. We're not going to have enough professors and teachers; we're going to go to the computer. This seems to me to change the whole concept that we've been discussing today.

DR. CHURCHMAN: Well, I'm an educator, and I agree. I think there are lots of things to be said and thought about on the part of the educational establishment. We have only scratched the surface. There's no question that, as Norm says, functionalism is taught in business schools.

But some of us who didn't grow up in business schools have always wondered why they teach the nonsense that they do in the functional fields. It isn't just the business schools that are at fault. Do you know what they do in the history of art department at Berkeley? They get 400 kids in a darkroom and show them a slide. Then the kids have to take down all the factual information about it—their examination consists of regurgitating a sample of that information. Why do academics go on doing that sort of thing? Who knows? But after all the challenge is fairly recent, and academics—like people in every other type of institution—are fairly good at taking care of challenges. If you're an optimist, you may care to hope that the educators will eventually begin to realize that educating the young is essentially not a fact-injecting device.

The real function of education, in my opinion, is to increase an individual's interest in learning. Fact injection tends to do just the opposite. So throughout our educational institutions there is a really basic feeling that we ought to be much more honest about what we're trying to do and realize that many of the things that have been done traditionally are not appropriate any more.

MR. REAM: I would just like to correct Wes. When I spoke of functionalization, I was referring not only to the business schools but to the whole educational field. I think what we've said is true of the schools of engineering as well. I believe that at this point we have not yet learned how to cross-fertilize; how to achieve interdisciplinary education or whatever you want to call it.

MR. BOETTINGER: Some critics have said that attempts at cross-fertilization have been cross-sterilization, and there has been evidence to support this. But I think we have a record of schedule adherence here that would gladden the heart of any manufacturer, and we don't want to be the ones to fault it. We've had a very stimulating experience; and, speaking for the panel, I want to say that none of us will go away unmindful of your charge.

I shall sum up briefly. It seems that we have arrived at two old questions. The first: What is the nature of man? We've called him a rational animal, a social animal, a tool-making animal, a playful animal. I submit that, to judge by our contemporaries, none of these definitions is exactly right. Probably the right appellation for man is *problem-solving animal*. And, if he's that, then we've certainly gotten a knapsack of ideas for further thought from this afternoon's discussion.

The other large question is the one that plagued the Romans: *"Sed quis custodiet ipsos custodes?"* as Juvenal asked. For those who went to Eton and Harrow, I'll translate that into "But who will guard the guards themselves?" This question has drifted through all our talk here. If we set up a system with all sorts of feedback and control, with all the "what if" questions already answered, who sets the average rate for the governor? That is still a question of value judgment. Dr. Barnett, as a liberal arts man, may get his hand on the big red handle, and all the other technicians will pull with the linkages, but the question still is not settled.

Opening Remarks

DR. ARTHUR W. ANGRIST
AFMR Vice President and Managing Director

This evening we have a panel discussion dealing with the behavioral sciences and their implications for management in the year 2000. We are privileged to have as our panel chairman Dr. S. C. Hollister, who has had a varied and distinguished career and has been the recipient of many honors. In addition to being dean emeritus of the Cornell University College of Engineering, he is a trustee of Cornell. But one thing which most of you perhaps are not aware of is a piece of information transmitted to me this afternoon in a telephone conversation with Dr. Hollister regarding his appearance here. I asked Dr. Hollister how I could correspond with him, and he said, "Just send anything to me at Hollister Hall." This was the first occasion that I'd had to speak with him, and he probably understood my quandary, for he explained, "You know, they named the new building after me because the students felt I ought to know where my office was."

We are very privileged to have with us this evening a man who has been active in the technical field, in the engineering field, in the educational field, and in the administrative field—but who is also a very keen observer and student of management. It is in this last capacity that he will conduct our panel session on the behavioral sciences and their impact on management of the future.

Panel: "Implications of the Behavioral Sciences on Management Practices in the Year 2000"

Chairman:

DR. S. C. HOLLISTER
Dean Emeritus, College of Engineering, Cornell University

Panel Members:

DR. BERNARD M. BASS
Director, Management Research Center, Graduate School of Business, University of Pittsburgh

DR. EDWIN R. HENRY
Professor, College of Business Administration, University of Rochester

DR. FORREST H. KIRKPATRICK
Vice President and Secretary, Wheeling Steel Corporation

Introduction by Dr. Hollister

We are in the midst of a review of managerial problems and their various implications for the year 2000. This is quite a long way ahead to look; it is not the kind of thing that engineers relish—a 33-year look is a pretty dim one. Budgets aren't made on any such terms, although sometimes long-term estimates are produced for bankers so as to get money to finance some of our endeavors. To be sure, we are attempting to make very much sharper evaluations and estimates in terms of the behavior of people. But those of us who have had experience with people in the classrooms know that they don't behave alike twice on the same day, to say nothing about different days. So to stretch our discussion out over a 33-year period is really quite an undertaking.

There was a time when we would have reversed the question that we're going to talk about tonight. We would have thought more in terms of managerial practices having an impact upon the behaviorial sciences; hence this reversal is a tribute to the behavioral sciences and the advances that they have made in recent years. It isn't very long ago that we didn't even talk about the behavioral sciences; we didn't use this kind of language. Yet they have made such vast gains lately that they have made a considerable contribution not only to management but to a host of other areas in the social structure. It is mandatory, therefore, that the behavioral sciences be thought about in terms of their effect on management 33 years from now.

We have a distinguished panel that is going to discuss this subject. Its members are psychologists—which I am not. They have an insight into the behavioral sciences as these are now practiced, and they also have the advantage of having had a lot of contact with management in industry and government. Two out of the three are predominantly connected with the academic scene, and the third is not without that taint, although not perhaps in the same degree. So we will see some reflection of what is happening on campus in our consideration of the behavioral sciences, as well as what goes on in management and in government insofar as the managerial function is concerned.

Our first panel speaker tonight will be Dr. Bass. He is professor of psychology and director of the Management Research Center at the University of Pittsburgh. He has been a visiting professor at the University of California at Berkeley, at Louisiana State University, and at the University of Navarra in Pamplona, Spain. He has lectured in a number of universities in the United States and Europe. He is the author of many research papers, as well as a number of leading books on psychology, one especially on organization in industry as it relates to psychological matters. Dr. Bass has served as consultant to a long list of industrial corporations. His special field relates to management and management development from a psychological standpoint.

I. Presentation by Dr. Bass

I am certain that I will be 33 years older in the year 2000. I am somewhat less certain about what the world of business and management will be like. I am least certain about what will be new in the behavioral sciences. As a consequence, I will offer few observations in the abstract about likely innovations in the behavioral sciences that may have an impact on management. To forecast relations between management and behavioral science in the year 2000, it will be more useful to look at what the world may be like then and to speculate from this to the interplay between the behavioral sciences on the one hand and management on the other.

FLEXIBLE ORGANIZATIONS

It seems to me that developments will continue in the understanding and skill with which we apply ourselves to the dynamics of organization change. The flexible organization will be the rule rather than the exception, and we will see more attention to both short- and long-range efforts by management to gear itself to a world of fairly continuous change. Internal mechanisms, feedback mechanisms, and training programs of various types that lead people to be flexible, to be ready for change, to be helpful in a changed process, are likely to be common in the year 2000.

Organizational designs are going to be multidimensional. We might envisage for the year 2000 organization charts which have in them one set of patterns for accountability, another set of patterns for information flow, and still another set of patterns for decision making. And the meshing of these multiple organizational designs will be a challenge for both management and the behavioral scientist. I expect that many of the latter will devote themselves in the years to come to laboratory experiments and simulations of various new proposed types of organizational forms.

IMPORTANCE OF CHALLENGING WORK

Other trends that look possible and have behavioral-science implications are inherent in our new approach to motivation—new in the sense that only in the past ten years have most psychologists reached a point where they now agree that some of the more important basic drives of man include information seeking and curiosity, along with such other primitive drives as hunger, thirst, and sex.

The inability of organisms to tolerate a complete lack of stimulation in the environment around them parallels the current interest in making jobs more challenging. I see an increasing tendency for management to work toward a life which will include more challenging jobs in a more stimulating environment.

So far as industry is concerned, this will probably result in salaries for all workers, coupled with rewards that are associated with challenging opportunities. Punishment will mean assignment to a boring job; rewards will come from chances at more stimulating kinds of work—at least at certain levels in the organization.

More of both sorts of new jobs—stimulating and boring—appear as we become more automated. The trend is toward both more simple jobs and more complex jobs with fewer in between in complexity. There is probably going to be increased bidding for the more complex jobs. In fact, it seems reasonable to expect someday that competition for more challenging work will replace competition for better salaries.

ON-LINE COMPUTERS

Earlier in this program, there was considerable emphasis on computerized displays and how they are going to affect decision-making processes. The on-line computing possibilities that are becoming available to management lead directly to dialogues between management and the computer. This already has begun; and, in the forth-coming years, we expect that the behavioral scientist will be able to provide further input which will make these dialogues between the manager and the computer more meaningful.

The speed with which communications flow into top management will be greatly increased. The executive will have the problems of coping with these speeded-up communications; of deciding when it is appropriate to simplify matters with a computer and when it is appropriate to try to deal with things himself.

As the manager attempts to simulate the environment, one of the big issues will be how much weight to give the computer in the total decision process. Is the manager to relegate the problem to the computer, or is he to make his decision primarily on the basis of the weight he attaches to the computer simulation and the assumptions that go into it? Is it his own personality that is going to be the determining factor? The question of how much computer and how much human judgment there is to be in the higher-level decision process should be an interesting one for at least the next 30 years.

MANAGEMENT EDUCATION

A world of 100 million managers has been envisaged by experts in international labor organizations—and why not? If you anticipate a world of 7 billion people, you must figure on needing a proportionate number of people to manage them. So it is rather obvious that we will need to package education techniques in a way that we are not doing now. The teacher, plus 20 students in a classroom, or one teacher and one student at the opposite ends of a log, is a clear impossibility. No matter what we think about packaged techniques, in order for even a small number of these 100 million managers to have an opportunity for managerial education, there will have to be great increases in programmed instruction, in television and video-tape innovations, in the use of small-group exercises of various types, in self-study techniques, in the simulation of workers and organizations, and in the effective confrontation of managers with simulated situations and environments.

SENSITIVITY TRAINING

Sensitivity training is likely to become a lot more proficient than it is now. In comparing some of my own experiences with this technique during the past decade, I am struck by what appear to be considerable increases in the efficiency with which it is conducted. Of course, the biggest problem that we still face is that of transferring the effects of sensitivity training from the laboratory to actual practice in the organization itself. Generally speaking, our success to date has been relatively low in this respect. It is to be expected that we will learn how to be more successful in the years to come.

THE MANAGER AS KNOWLEDGE WORKER

Management is becoming increasingly an intellectual process featuring rational planning, mathematization of decision making, and systematic problem solving. Now the manager processes information as blue collar employees process materials. He is a knowledge worker. His interest is likely to grow in the psychology of problem solving and decision making. In the future, I expect an accentuation of these trends.

Intellectual processes will be of greater importance to the future manager than to his present-day counterpart; he will spend more time on them. The managerial job will have many more intellectual and educational requirements. It will involve more technical scientific and engineering problems, as well as more complex budgeting and financial decisions. The manager will be functioning in a world where his performance will be evaluated even more than it is today on his intellectual skills in bringing about increases in rate of growth, in quality of services and output.

If the computer prognosticators are right, upper-level managers will be involved in fewer day-to-day decisions—decisions that can be programmed for the computer. As a result, they will be less involved in "fire fighting"; rather, they will be more scholarly, able, and more willing to take intellectual, generalized views of the business environment with which they must deal. At the same time, they will face increasingly intricate technologies, organizational forms, and marketing phenomena again which places a premium on intellectual prowess.

INCREASED FOCUS ON BEHAVIORAL SCIENCES BY MANAGERS

Like many other graduate business schools, the Graduate School of Business at the University of Pittsburgh has opted to make a heavy investment of student time in study of the behavioral sciences. The investment seems to be paying off. In a follow-up survey of MBA graduates of the 1961–1966 classes, respondents singled out courses in the behavioral sciences as among the most valuable to them on the job. Probably the most obvious and most general kind of statement that can be made safely is that managers are going to be big users of whatever behavioral sciences happen to be around in the year 2000.

The manager in the year 2000 will be seeking out information about people, about different kinds of people, about different cultures, about different styles of living. This will be even more important for the manager than it is today in the sense that the world of the future will contain within it more managers who are pursuing—or attempting to pursue—democratic and permissive rather than authoritarian methods. They will have to know more about people in order to be successful in this respect.

More managers will see themselves in teacher roles vis-à-vis their subordinates. The teacher-manager whose evaluation will depend to some extent on how much he develops his subordinates will become more commonplace. And community leadership will be expected of a manager. I noticed in today's paper a strong message offering support from General Motors management to the mayor of Detroit, indicating that the company's resources are available to aid in Detroit's post-riot rebuilding. Managers and their organizations will involve themselves in community problem solving much more in the future than in the past. The broad-gauge manager-citizen will certainly be of greater significance in the year 2000 than he is today.

Other areas of environmental change will call for the manager to be knowledgeable about behavioral and social problems, social change, and particularly cross-cultural and intercultural matters. Foreign markets are growing faster than domestic markets. It has been suggested that 60 percent of all the world's business will eventually be done by international firms. Tariffs are likely to be lower; there will be more countries in common markets. Capitalist and socialist ideologies will have come closer together; the typical American manager will have to face up to a world of mixed economies, not necessarily like his own, in the many countries in which he will do business.

The trend toward devoting a greater proportion of national income to health, education, and welfare will continue. The businessman either is going to be a very frustrated person or will necessarily acquire an appreciation of the society in which he lives and its problems which will require 21-century solutions.

Managers will be more willing and able to transfer from business to hospitals, to government, to research foundations, and back again. In doing so, they will be likely to seek and keep up with a wide spectrum of information about sociology, psychology, social issues, cultural matters, and political affairs. Correspondingly, behavioral scientists will increase their efforts to help make this information available to managers. Magazines and journals exist now that were not available five years ago—for example, *Transaction* and *Psychology Today*. Highly readable, they present in digested form the current findings of the behavioral sciences. It is likely that there will be an increase in this kind of communication, making possible a more rapid dissemination of behavioral science information to managers.

DR. HOLLISTER: I seem to have heard Dr. Bass say that management is going to be much more involved by the year 2000. A manager is going to have to know a whole lot more than he does now, and he's supposed to know a great deal about other things than management even now. So we're going to have an educational problem just to train managers. And one of the questions which I hope will be raised later is the extent to which management will be followed as a kind of technique quite independent of the company or organization to which it's being applied, so that it can be lifted off, in a manner of speaking, and used in another organization with equal facility.

Our next speaker will be Dr. Edwin R. Henry. Like Dr. Bass, he earned his Ph.D. at Ohio State University, but I believe at a very much different time.

DR. HENRY: A few years' difference!

DR. HOLLISTER: Dr. Henry spent about 12 years as professor of psychology at New York University; then, for four years, he was chief of personnel research in the Adjutant General's Office of the U.S. War Department. His experience in industry includes 20 years as manager of the Social Science Research Division, Standard Oil Company (New Jersey), which is a firm that most of us Easterners are familiar with, and two years as director of selection in the Peace Corps. Since 1965, he has been professor in the College of Business at the University of Rochester, in New York State, and a consultant to the Richardson Foundation in Greensboro, North Carolina. He has written numerous articles in scientific journals. Dr. Henry has had, as you see, a mixture of academic and practical experience in applying the principles of psychology.

II. Presentation by Dr. Henry

I was going to start out with a story, but I think I'll skip it. If I'd told the story, I'd have made it the one about the eminent personality visiting a penitentiary in Texas. He saw a very old man there, and he went up to the old man and asked, "How long have you been in here?" "About two years." "What are you in for?" "Rape." "How old are you?" "Ninety-two." "Were you guilty?" "No, but the charge sounded so good I pleaded guilty."

Now, if I had started out with that story, I would have gone on to say something else. Hearing President Barnett today warn us about the trouble we can get into by making predictions made me decide to make some. They're based on some assumptions which I believe are tenable, especially after reading this morning's *Wall Street Journal* and seeing all the mergers contemplated, approved, suggested, or awaiting approval and looking at the picture of American industry over the past few years, which implies that 33 years from now there will probably be many more big companies (and by big I mean *really* big) because they're much more efficient than small organizations. Small organizations are going to have to become big, either to get capital gains or to become efficient. So I am assuming that during the next 33 years this trend is likely to continue and that we will see the emergence of more big, efficient, cost-reducing, public-service kinds of organizations than we've had in the past.

I'm also assuming that this is going to hold true of government, education, the charitable foundations, all so-called nonprofit businesses; and that there are some consequences that will follow. I would therefore like to present five propositions. Three of them I don't have much to say about, but the other two I would really like to try to exploit. These propositions are as follows:

1. The management process in good, effective organizations 33 years from now will be no different from the management process in good, effective organizations today.
2. The organizations over which the good managers in the year 2000 will be presiding will be quite different from comparable good organizations now.
3. The same kinds of men who are good managers now will be the good managers in the year 2000.
4. The technical knowledge and skills acquired through formal education and specific job-related experience which will be required of the good manager in the year 2000 will be quite different than it is now.
5. In the year 2000, as now, there will be a terrific shortage of good managers, and the processes and facilities for their development will be quite different from those that exist now.

1. THE MANAGEMENT PROCESS

First let's talk about proposition No. 1. The management process in which the effective manager engages today is essentially one of supplying leadership. I know that the Harvard Business School talks about delegation, accountability, and all that sort of thing, but the essential job of the effective manager of the present, as of the effective manager in 2000, is one of supplying leadership.

I think the manager will continue to be the kind of person who uses a staff to develop plans and alternative solutions to problems or alternative decisions to be made for his consideration—that is, to help him arrive at the decision to be made—but the manager will still have to make the decision himself. I believe that the effective manager 33 years from now is going to be the one who, under the general policies and guidance of the absentee owners and his board of directors, will be able to translate their goals and their desires into organizational goals which he and his organization can effectively carry out. I'm speaking generally of top management, but the same thing will be true among managers down the line; the goals established by higher echelons must be translated into operational goals for lower echelons. To do so, the top manager cannot escape delegating both authority and responsibility for action; hence one of his big jobs, as now, is going to be checking the performance of both individuals and organizational units. He will, as the effective manager does now, not try to handle the routine day-to-day decisions that have to be made, but will manage by exception, because, if a decision can be made on the basis of logic or fact, it can be made better by a computer than by him. *His* job is to make the decisions where there are no logical rules or facts.

Finally, something else that's going to be true in 2000 as it is right now is that we stockholders are going to demand of the managers of that time effectiveness in developing personnel and management succession. In short, I don't think there's any case to be made for the management *process*'s being any different from what it is now.

2. THE ORGANIZATION

The organization over which Mr. Manager 2000 will preside is, however, likely to be quite different. I base this statement on the kind of research which the behavioral sciences have been developing for the past 20 years or so and which indicates that organizations are becoming more participative. There's less of the boss handing down a decision and more of people from several echelons arriving at alternative decisions from among which the boss chooses. (Incidentally, did you ever hear that old gag about "What is 'boss' spelled backward?" Answer: "He's a double S.O.B.")

Organizations will be more democratic in the year 2000, they will demand more cooperation, they will require more highly skilled people and at the same time very many more people with lesser skills than predominate in organizations today. There are going to be more limited numbers of people who can be promoted through the ranks to top management; organizations may have to become less career-minded and promotion-from-within-minded than they have been up to the present. This last, which is perhaps an aside, I base on our current emphasis on discrimination, civil rights, and that sort of thing. I think there is going to be a growing demand that we employ people in entry-level jobs whether they can be promoted to higher-level jobs or not. Heretofore, we have tried to hire people who will be good enough on the entry level that they will be "promotion material," but now the criterion is going to change and we are going to employ people who can be expected to perform only the entry-level jobs satisfactorily.

The real issue here is going to be one of discrimination. Sure, we're going to discriminate in employment, in promotion, in any personnel actions. But what we're going to have to prove in the future is that we're not discriminating on the basis of irrelevant variables. I personally know of only one instance of relevant discrimination on the basis of race: it does absolutely no good for the Arabian American Oil Company to hire a Jew because he cannot get into Saudi Arabia.

3. THE GOOD MANAGERS

To repeat: The same kinds of people who are the effective managers today will be the effective managers in effective organizations in the year 2000.

I've been plagued over a period of years, in attempting to do studies on the identification of managerial potential, by the alibi that, well, it doesn't really do any good to study our organization now because 20 years from now we're going to require different kinds of people to manage this organization, and how do we know that the kinds that are successful today are going to be successful 20 years from now? The answer is, we don't know.

This is the same alibi that I heard 33 years ago. I submit that the people who started fresh out of college 33 years ago and became today's top management were bright people—but there are lots of ineffective, unsuccessful managers who are bright too. The successful men had high scholastic ratings in college, but so did many of the others. The successful men were ambitious, but the rest had ambitions too.

There *are* differences between the managers who have gotten to the top and the ones who didn't. These can be defined in terms of the creativeness, the innovativeness, and the tolerance for innovativeness in an organization. I've heard it said a great many times that the only man who can be an innovator in a particular organization is the boss—don't ever try to be one if you want to stay here, because the one thing he can't tolerate is creative people. But not only have effective managers got to tolerate change; they're the people who 33 years ago started *planning* change, who *engineered* change, who were *change agents* in their organizations, who have made those organizations very different from what they were in 1934.

I see no evidence whatsoever for assuming that these same kinds of people will not continue to innovate, plan, engineer, and become the agents for change in the next 33 years. As a stockholder, I hope that the corporations in which I own shares will elect the same kinds of people to manage them that have been managing them for the past 33 years. In the year 2000 we're going to want organizations that have made the same kind of progress they have to date.

There are a couple of other things about effective managers for which we don't have very much evidence. I mean the hard kind of evidence that researchers like to get their fingers into. However, a few findings have developed out of some widely known research over the past few years, and these do discriminate between the effective and the less effective managers of today. One of the most important of these is that the more effective managers are the ones who have set high standards of performance for their organizational units and for individuals in those units. They have performed outstandingly themselves, and they have demanded that kind of performance of their organizations. Also, the more effective managers of today gave evidence of being more mature—and independent—than most people of their age, or they did things that we would say constituted more mature, independent behavior, earlier than the less effective managers did. And, despite William H. Whyte, Jr., there is plenty of evidence that they have generally been friendlier, more socially acceptable, and more unorthodox and less organization-minded than their less effective colleagues. If I were to give a piece of advice to a youngster today, it is that he read *The Organization Man*. Then, if he'll answer all the questions in the book, not as Mr. Whyte advises, but in exactly the opposite way, he'll get that job he wants with the good corporation!

4. TECHNICAL KNOWLEDGE AND SKILL

It is self-evident that the technical knowledge and skill required for job success will be quite different, and after this afternoon's panel discussion you know that. The content of the courses that people take in college to prepare for managerial jobs is going to change. It will not be any more difficult than it was 33 years ago, but it will employ new vocabularies and some new concepts. Similarly, the job-related experience which is going to be required of managers in the year 2000 will be very different to be in tune with the new technology. But the managerial behavior required will not be different.

5. MANAGEMENT DEVELOPMENT

In the past, managerial development has rested on a belief in the emergence theory. You hire a group of college graduates, you put them on the job, and out of that group you hope will emerge a few leaders who will manage and lead the organization in the future. But, with computers between the lower levels of supervision and the top levels of management making the decisions that middle management now makes, the question is going to be, how do you get promising young college new-hires around the computer phase (which could kill them) and into top management where they can be effective? I once heard an eminent chairman of the board say that his company had the greatest program for developing promotable managers of any organization in the world. The one thing that was missing was a program for teaching people, once they were promoted, to leave the old job behind them and not become a cork in the bottleneck of progress. Now, with the computer, maybe they won't cork things up.

Last but not least, with the shortage of managerial talent which is

Lawrence A. Appley, President of AMA and AFMR,
standing beside the oil painting of the late
Donald W. Mitchell

Dr. Arthur W. Angrist, Vice President and Managing Director of AFMR

Donald G. Mitchell, Chairman, Board of Directors and Executive Committee, AMA

Guests in the Donald W. Mitchell Memorial Library

Mr. Appley, on the Flag Terrace, dedicating the Manager Learning Center

Dr. Lillian M. Gilbreth, life member of AMA and charter member of AFMR

Merritt L. Kastens, Director of the AFMR Manager Learning Center

*The Chandelier Room of the
AFMR Manager Learning
Center*

Photos by
Richard Broussard

*The Time Capsule,
containing records of
current management
practices, to be opened
August 22, 2000*

undoubtedly going to become more acute, we must identifiy potential managers earlier in their careers. We must abandon the concept
of emergence through survival in the organization and plan a management development program based on the individual needs of people
who show promise of advancing to the top management ranks. This
is something which, if I hadn't used up all my time already, I'd like
to spend about an hour talking about. It is that important.

DR. HOLLISTER: The last speaker on the panel will be Dr. Forrest H.
Kirkpatrick. At one time he was in charge of personnel and labor relations for the Radio Corporation of America in New York City. For
some years he was professor and dean at Bethany College; later he
was visiting professor at Columbia, the University of Pittsburgh, and
New York University. He is a member of the board of governors of
the University of West Virginia, a member of the West Virginia Commission on Higher Education, and president of the Council of
Wheeling College.

Dr. Kirkpatrick has been associated with Wheeling Steel Corporation since 1946. In 1952 he became a corporate officer. He is now the
company's vice president and secretary.

III. Presentation by Dr. Kirkpatrick

In *The Future as History*, by Robert Heilbroner, the striking point is made that change is now so dynamic a component of
our society that past history is of no great importance in predicting
the future. This means that the history of importance is the history
of tomorrow. This discussion, therefore, of management as an art and
science in the 30 or 40 years ahead seems wise and appropriate. The
pull of the year 2000 may prove to be much more important than the
"prologue" of the year 1900.

With the invention of the wheel, a revolutionary new partnership was born—*man and machine*. Some say that this was the origin
of automation—an accelerating process of shifting more of the work-
load from human effort to mechanical effort. With all the new man-

agement tools now available in the fields of communication and analysis, a new kind of partnership is being created which seems to portend even more striking ramifications. This might be called the partnership of *management and machine.*

This new partnership, as it develops over the next 30 or 40 years, can extend enormously the capabilities of managers—not at an arithmetic rate, but at a geometric rate. The body of knowledge available to management decision makers today is infinitely greater than it was just a few years ago, and we can only guess what it will be in the years ahead. The recording, the classification, and the appropriate recall of needed information have already gone far, far beyond the ability of the unaided individual.

In the process of decision making itself, the analysis of increasingly complex alternatives can be vastly simplified and thus the quality of the decision greatly improved. Management decisions now being made on hunch will, in the near future, be made with precision and confidence and with full knowledge of known facts, alternatives, and probabilities.

This new partnership of management and machine will, in due time, cause drastic changes in the way business enterprises are organized. Businesses have been forced to grow larger and larger in order to meet ever greater problems and challenges. But more recently, in order to get the decision making process as close to the input data as possible, our business enterprises have been decentralizing themselves. In the process, lower and lower levels of supervision have been given the responsibility and dignity of decision making. Definitive and sometimes arbitrary boundaries have been established around each decision-making point, setting up so-called accountability centers to determine results and to provide incentives for the making of good decisions.

With improved computer techniques a top manager now can have available facts, choices, and analytical methods far, far beyond the perspective of a lower-level supervisor—even information about the very business or production processes directed by the supervisor himself. There is a growing possibility that the computers may soon be telling us that these "accountability centers" as a technique are wasteful. While maximizing the profit of a particular center, management may be depriving the overall organization of far more profit than the benefit accruing to an individual center. More information by way of the computers sometimes makes it clear that the business enterprise is composed of many little individual businesses replete with duplication, conflicts, and lack of overall perspective.

All this suggests that a new trend—"recentralization"—is about to be born in the basic structure of business enterprises in order to take better advantage of the broad view of the organization now made possible by the new partnership of management and machine. This kind of pyramidic organization structure could, in the future, provide fewer and fewer opportunities for the individual to have a sense of purpose and a place in the sun. In the overall process there is the danger of depersonalizing the business enterprise as well as its inhabitants. Here, then, is an area where the behavioral sciences can provide insight and guidance.

NEEDED: A BALANCED COMBINATION

Let us remember that human beings live for more than survival and that, as we come closer and closer to the year 2000, we shall see man's material needs pretty well fulfilled. This means that the other strong appetites of man will become increasingly important. Man's craving for self-expression, for self-fulfillment, and for the self-satisfaction of knowing that he is contributing something of value to his society is very strong.

Standing squarely between the forces of economic efficiency and technological development and the irresistible psychological and sociological pressures of the human spirit are the representatives of management. The manager must be a technologist and a psychologist, an engineer and a sociologist, a man who is analytical and reflective, and a man of action—but a man who is deliberate before action. The new manager must indeed be a rare and a *balanced* combination of scientist and humanist!

The new manager will realize that his enterprise needs the innovations that only human intelligence and effort can supply. Computers can do some very fantastic things; but they do not innovate, they do not design, they do not invent, and they do not dream. Under the competitive, speeded-up activity of tomorrow's business enterprise, the thrust of innovation and invention will have great and unique value.

PROJECTED ORGANIZATIONAL PATTERN

If all that we know about the behavioral sciences is synthesized into a new organization structure, internally consistent but radically different, we might find ourselves in the midst of something rather far removed from what is common in business and industry today. I wonder if the organization pattern in the year 2000 will include the following:

Eliminating the Superior-Subordinate Relationship. If the authoritarian hierarchy with its superior-subordinate pairing is to be removed, it must be replaced by another form of discipline and control. This substitute could be individual self-discipline arising from the self-interest created by a competitive market mechanism. Perhaps the individual would even negotiate, as a free agent, a continuously changing structure of relationships with those with whom he exchanges goods and services.

Establishing Individual Decision Centers. Within the new organization each man or small team (partnership) could be a decision center responsible for the success of those activities in which the center chooses to emerge. The decision center concept in this instance would be very different from the budget concept which is so common in financial planning and control. In the budget center the individual governs himself relative to a negotiated expenditure rate. The budget measures performance in terms of cost compared to accomplishment. In contrast, rewards at the decision center, both financial and psychological, would depend on profit in the broad sense and not on expenditure rate.

Keeping Policy Free and Easy. Policy would allow freedom to innovate and would have the fewest restrictions compatible with the coordination needed to insure overall strength, stability, and growth. Policy would be accessible, clear, and not retroactive. The source of policy would be a process that insures some consensus by those affected and that provides for the common good. Policies would be consistent by virtue of being designed as parts of a total policy structure. Policy making would be separated from the distractions of operational decision making; otherwise, short-term pressures might usurp time from policy creation.

Providing Adequate Information. On-line use of computers for both data processing and internal communication could provide an information picture that would be up to date and fully processed at all times. Partially processed inventories of information could be substantially reduced, along with the internal communication needed to estimate conditions. With a well-managed system, adequate information could be directly accessible to persons who now operate with too little information. If internal communication could be improved, energy could be turned to the even more challenging quest for external information—information about new technical developments, new management methods, new employees, customer services, product performance in the field, and changing markets.

Balancing Reward and Risk. Such an organization would retain and combine the advantages of earlier organizational forms while minimizing their disadvantages. So often we wish we could combine the stability and strength of the large, diversified business organization with the more direct challenge and opportunity that the small company offers. It goes without saying that we must avoid the stifling bureaucracy and compartmentalization that are frequent in large organizations where a central power holds the right to allocate resources and make decisions.

This type of organization, in contrast to the conventional corporation, would allow the individual to have greater ease of voluntary exit, but perhaps would exercise more restraint over entry. It would hold people because they want to be a part of this kind of enterprise. Any rights of deferred compensation, earned by past performance, should be readily transportable if the individual does decide to leave.

Enhancing the Rights of the Individual. Considering the emerging concepts of social justice, some people have doubts as to the moral right of stockholders, acting through management, to hold arbitrary power over individual employees. Perhaps by the year 2000 a new organization could be developed around a "constitution" that established the rights of the individual and the limitation of power the organization would have over him. Corporate policy would be subject to constitutional provisions just as the U.S. Constitution has supremacy over laws made by national legislative bodies. To complete the system, there would have to be means for "judicial review" by impartial tribunals to arbitrate disagreements and to interpret the operational meaning of the constitution and policies.

Keeping Education in the Forefront. In such an organization, education would serve three purposes not essential in an authoritarian corporate government. It would release the strengths and resources of each individual through persistent training and retraining, it would perhaps encourage noninvolvement, and it would orient employees to the world community with its many cultures and opportunities. Let me say that I am increasingly concerned over the trend to demand complete involvement on the part of all participants by any corporate organization or enterprise. Perhaps we would do better to recognize that man has many needs: some that are fulfilled by his participation in the business organization; some that are fulfilled by other means such as community and civic work, educational agencies, churches, social groups, and families; and some that will not be fulfilled but will be powerful motivators to higher levels of achievement.

There are other characteristics of such an organization that should be mentioned—some even more important than those I have cited. I have tried only to suggest the pattern. I recognize that it may sound like a dream or fantasy, but someday someone will try something like it. A promising and reasonable approach would be to build a new organization from the ground up in the new pattern. It might be either a truly new and independent organization or a detached and isolated subsidiary of an existing corporation. It should feel its way, make modifications where necessary, and create success at each stage as a foundation for future growth.

PROBLEMS AND CONCERNS

It is well to remind ourselves that acquiring the technical capacity to automate production as fully as we wish, or as we find economical, means that per-capita capacity to produce will ultimately continue to increase far beyond the point where any justification will remain for poverty or deprivation. The means to rule out scarcity as mankind's first problem will be within reach by the year 2000, and then we shall have time to attend to other problems.

A new and different pattern of concerns may develop. Men may get interested in educational and cultural goals, in enlarging the "good" of the "good life." This could mean another renaissance with our national concerns centered about art, literature, music, and philosophy. Or science, with the emphasis on health, might be even more of a basic national concern than now.

Let me add now that, in spite of the increased productivity, the occupations that men in the year 2000 will find in business and industry will be fairly familiar ones. And I am sure we can dismiss the "R.U.R. fear"—that is, the fear that many people feel at the prospect of fraternizing with robots in an automated world. Fraternize we shall, but in the friendly, familiar way that we now fraternize with our power shovels, our automobiles, and our electric stoves.

Five other problems in particular must receive a great deal of attention as we move toward the year 2000: (1) utilizing leisure time, (2) learning more about genetics and population control, (3) developing a science of man, (4) finding alternatives for work and production as basic goals for society, and (5) reformulating man's view of his place in the universe. There are other problems too, like those referred to in this program—better management, better education, and better government. The vast potentialities of technology and science as substitutes for human work are clear. The research now going on in the behavioral sciences is equally important for understanding how humans perform information-processing tasks; that is, how they think. That kind of behavioral research has already made major progress toward a psychology of cognitive processes, and there are reasons to hope that research will not be limited to cognition but will extend to the affective aspects of behavior as well. This kind of research may make it possible for the world of 2000 to have behavioral theories that are as successful as the theories we have in chemistry and biology today. Anyway, we shall have a much better understanding of the nature of human nature. This has obvious and fundamental consequences for overall management and for specific situations.

The continuing rise in productivity may produce profound changes, in addition to those already evident, in the role that work plays in man's life and among man's goals. It is hard to believe that man's appetite for gadgets can continue to expand at the rate required to keep work and production in central roles in the society. Even John K. Galbraith's proposal for diverting expenditures from gadgets to social services can be only a temporary expedient. Before long we shall have to come to grips with the problem of leisure.

In today's society, the corporation satisfies important social and psychological needs in addition to the needs for goods and services. For those who do well in managerial careers, it satisfies needs for success and status. For some of these men and for others it is one of the important outlets for creativity. In a society where scarcity of goods and services is of little importance, those institutions—including the corporation—whose main function is to deal with scarcity will occupy a less important place than they have in the past.

Success in management in the year 2000 will carry smaller rewards in prestige and status than it now does. Moreover, as the decision-making function becomes more highly automated, corporate decision making will perhaps provide fewer outlets for creative drives than it now does. Alternative outlets will have to be supplied.

It is only one step from the problem of goals to what used to be called "cosmology" and is now referred to by psychiatrists as the "identity crisis." The developing capacity of computers to simulate man—and thus both to serve as his substitute and to provide a theory of human mental functions—will change man's conception of his own identity as a species. The definition of man's uniqueness has always formed the kernel of his cosmological and ethical systems. With Copernicus and Galileo he ceased to be the species located at the center of the universe, attended by sun and stars. With Darwin he ceased to be the species specially created and specially endowed by God with soul and reason. With Freud he ceased to be the species whose behavior was governable by a conscious, rational mind. As we begin to produce mechanisms that think and learn or come close to it, man may cease to be the species uniquely capable of complex, intelligent manipulation of his environment.

I am confident, however, that man will, as he has in the past, find a new way of describing his place in the universe—a way that, while different from the present one, will satisfy his needs for dignity, for purpose, and for a continuing look at the stars.

DR. HOLLISTER: We'll consider this to be the seventh inning and stand up for a short stretch before we subject the panel to questions from the floor. I'm sure by this time you've had a lot of provocative thoughts you would like to exchange with the panel members. If you want to address a question directly to one of the panel and call him by name, that is all right. If you just want to toss out a question—

DR. KIRKPATRICK: You say call him a name?

DR. HOLLISTER: You can do it either way. The floor is open.

Discussion

DR. GILBRETH: Mr. Chairman, could I make a few comments?

DR. HOLLISTER: Please do, Mrs. Gilbreth.

DR. GILBRETH: I have listened with a great deal of interest, as I know you all did, to these three talks. I think on the whole they're very encouraging because they really show us we still have something to do. It would be dreadful if all the problems were solved, wouldn't it? It is very evident that they are not.

I do think, however, that we are making some not so very well known but really great contributions in these days. Some time ago, meeting a young man I knew quite well, I asked how he was getting on with his work. He was going abroad for his company, and visiting the people in his organization who were overseas. He said, "I've had a queer experience. My company sent me to see one of our subsidiaries over there, and I found out that the way in which they were doing things was not what we'd been doing but, it seemed to me, very much better for them. But, if I go back and turn that report in, my company will think I'm very superficial. "I think that's going to be an interesting test of your company," I told him. "If it were *my* company, and it acted like that, it wouldn't be my company the next day. I'd be out."

I didn't see the young man for quite a while. When we met again much later, he told me, "My company thought that my report was perfectly fair and that we should carry through. But," he said, "something new has happened." "What *could* happen?" I asked. And the young man said, "Why, *we* are doing things the way they do them overseas." It was really an experience to learn that something of that sort can happen.

It seems to me that the impetus is spreading all through the world. Think how small the world really is getting. Think how quickly—more quickly each year—you can climb on board a jet, dart through the sky, and in no time at all be in another place.

A particularly encouraging thing—and we do need a few encouraging things—is what the Peace Corps is doing. It's doing very much better than most of us would have thought it possibly could. It has had to learn the hard way. The first groups I saw go abroad I thought were going more or less as do-gooders. It is true that they wanted to do *something*; but they were insistent, really, on trying to help people to become exactly like us. As I listened to some of them, I wondered what kind of contribution these people seriously thought they could make. But times have changed. Not very long ago, I met a group of about 40, I think, just out of college, with the wives. I wished I could talk with them for a long while because I was amazed to see the amount and variety of work that these men in training could do; they were not only exploring the kinds of jobs they had been assigned but trying to invent others.

In any case, if we are going to send overseas the best people we have, and I think we should, we have to be very sure that when they come back we don't have the experience that many and many a faculty member has had. "Yes," says the returned Peace Corps or big-corporation recruit, "I wanted to help, but the organization isn't at all interested, really." Let's look at the future boldly—encourage those who are making the things we have outlined happen. These next years are really going to be thrilling ones. I don't think we'll see all the changes that have been forecast, but we will see many of them.

QUESTION: I would like Dr. Kirkpatrick to expand a little on the possible role of labor in the future. He alluded to this briefly. In some countries of Europe, labor now enters into top management decisions.

DR. KIRKPATRICK: Are you talking about organized labor, or are you talking about the individual employee? They are two different things, you know.

QUESTIONER: Well, I'm not sure how it works.

DR. KIRKPATRICK: In Europe, of course, the labor unions are very powerful; they are represented on companies' boards of directors. But what I was alluding to was individual employees' being treated in this new boss-employee relationship, not the recognition of organized labor as a force.

I think the power of organized labor will diminish by the year 2000. It's being kept alive pretty much by the politicians rather than by the union members themselves. If it weren't for the strong support that our political leaders are getting from the unions, they would by the very fact of their ineffectiveness in plants be less important even today. By the year 2000, we'll have no more unions. We'll have Walter Reuther and people like that in the Hall of Fame, but they'll be long forgotten—like the inventor of the threshing machine!

QUESTION: Dr. Bass, you described our society in the year 2000 very much as though managers would be operating like Renaissance princes, like the Medici, all involved in a tremendous amount of social activity. But somehow or another you didn't seem to emphasize the most important thing: making a buck. I wonder whether that was by design or default?

DR. BASS: I'm not sure. I would expect that the typical manager in the year 2000 would see himself as a member of an institution that's going to survive for another 5,000 years; and, in order for it to survive, it will have to see itself as part of a bigger system. Making money will be important, but making money at the expense of ending up without any institutions to manage will not be.

Consider air pollution. Probably there will be some managers who will strive honestly to join in the overall effort toward voluntary reduction of the air pollution caused by their own plants. But no doubt, over time, it will be government intervention that will lead to really effective air-pollution control. The problem for management will be to maintain a willingness to cooperate as government, representing society, develops a plan for all industry in a given area.

I guess my main point, using air pollution as an example, is that management will have to be cognizant of the fact that its own institution is part of a bigger system. Managers will be princes in the sense that they will have to negotiate even more than they do now with other large organizations and agencies. The world will be more tightly regulated; many people won't think very kindly of the prospect, but 2000 will be a year of greater regulation rather than the year 1968. In the year 2000 making a buck will be important, but it will be making a buck within a more highly regulated world than we have now.

VOICE FROM AUDIENCE: I'm reminded of the story that Thomas J. Bata, a long-standing supporter of AMA who heads the worldwide Bata Shoe Company, told us right here about a manager of theirs in Germany. The general manager, while vacationing in France, noted that the French manager had changed the paint on all his doors to a most effective new color. So he went back to Germany and painted all *his* doors. When Tom found out about it, they had already fired the man in France because he used the color which was copied!

I also have been reflecting that Pepsi-Cola in England has an entirely different design on its can from the one that is used in this country. It will be interesting to see whether, as suggested, the hint will be taken over here.

But I really wanted to say that Dr. Kirkpatrick might have thought he was being asked to project us into 3000 rather than 2000. He touched on language. Nobody knows how many languages there are in the world—over 3000, I think. I first studied Italian at Ohio State University about 1920, have since become practically bilingual in Spanish, and have managed to learn a couple of other languages as well. But if, in highly concentrated societies like Belgium and Switzerland, you can't get people who live five miles apart to speak each other's languages, I think it's a hopeless dream in this country. What's more, I don't really see much need for the Oklahoma or the Kansas farm boy to learn French or Italian when the odds are that he will never get farther east than St. Louis, if that.

I've thought quite a great deal about this subject. In fact, I've made quite a study of languages—took a course at New York University just last winter—and I despair that any very considerable number of people will ever become bilingual or even reasonably proficient in a second language. Why? Simply because they lack the motivation. Goodness knows you do have this motivation in so many other countries; but, when I first went to Spain 30 years ago, I had to translate what the fellow from Galicia said for the fellow from Seville, and it's still that way.

DR. KIRKPATRICK: I'll settle for English. If we'll start speaking that, it will be a great help!

MR. MITCHELL: [1] I am no good at languages, but I have traveled around the world a good bit and I anticipate an automatic handling of this language situation. I no longer see any need, on our part, for learning a second language, and I no longer see any need for Esperanto. That's a thing of the past. English has become the universal language of the world; when AMA gives presidents' courses in Italy, Switzerland, Sweden, Belgium, or anywhere else for that matter, I seldom notice a man pick up an earphone to get the simultaneous translation into English, French, Italian, German, or whatever. When he does listen in, it's only to see whether the translation is any good, not because he doesn't understand the speaker. I'm told that in the middle management seminars the simultaneous translation is still utilized, but at the presidents' level it's not.

Another thing is this. When, as I go around the world, I try my halting French on a Frenchman, he smiles and speaks English to me. He would much rather try his English out on me than have me try my French out on him—and he does have a motive. English is the business language of the world, and he wants to show that he's conversant in it. It's my opinion that by the year 2000 a businessman who speaks English will have no language problem whatever. Everybody in every country of the world he goes to will speak English to him without reservation. Now, I don't condone this. I think we *ought* to learn somebody else's language, but the fact is that we don't have to. He learns *our* language.

DR. HENRY: If you picked anything but French, I would possibly agree with you, but I never knew a Frenchman who, with the slightest hint that you spoke a few words of French, would spontaneously burst into English because he wanted to practice.

MR. MITCHELL: I have been in a lawyer's office; and, when the man heard my French, he couldn't stand it. "Talk English!" he said.

[1] Don G. Mitchell, Chairman of the Board, AMA, and Chairman of the Board, General Time Corporation.

DR. HENRY: Did it ever occur to you, though, that if you hadn't tried to speak his language, he wouldn't have spoken yours?

MR. MITCHELL: He wanted to show me how much better he spoke my language than I do his.

DR. HENRY: Yes, but unless you tried to speak his language, he wouldn't have cared two hoots about you in English.

VOICE FROM AUDIENCE: I have a question; but first, if I may, I'd like to address myself to this question of languages. I'm sure everyone in this room will agree that a multilingual damn fool is still a damn fool. Those of us who work in international trade and hire on the basis of language capability frequently make a mistake because, if a man has nothing to say, it doesn't matter how many languages he can say it in. If we really wanted to build our business on multilinguality, we should hire the head waiters of the world; they all speak five languages and dress impeccably—and you don't have to pay them, you just tip them handsomely.

However, it would be a sad world indeed if we didn't make an effort to be multilingual. It is true, as Don Mitchell said, that we talk to presidents now in English because of an inability on our part, not theirs. But we can't talk to foremen, we can't talk to our workers, we can't find out what's in their hearts when they speak a language that isn't native to them. Even in the United Nations, the interpreters translate simultaneously only into their own native language because that's the only one that comes quickly to them. They call that their primary language. Even a man who is bilingual in French and English, if French was the first language he learned, will translate only into French because that's the only reliable way.

Many years ago, when I was serving at our embassy in Vienna, we had some families who were constantly changing household help. This meant a great impairment of the efficiency of the officer concerned because his wife was never happy: into one house, out of the house, get a maid, the maid's gone, get a *Kindermädchen*, the *Kindermädchen's* gone—and, even though she's not to call him on the phone at the embassy, she does. So, as an experiment, we once prepared two charts. One showed the language ability of the wife; the other, the number of changes of domestic help. When the first chart was superimposed on the second, they looked as though they had both been turned out on the same printing press.

I would like to submit a test of language skills that I have found very effective in my own work. If I'm employing a man for work in international trade based in the United States, the only requirement—and it isn't always easy to find—is that he speak and understand English. However, if we station him in a country that doesn't have too difficult a language (I would except Finland and Hungary and Japan because these have extremely difficult languages), and if he lives in that country for two years and still doesn't have a working knowledge of that language, we say, "Come home, boy. You don't really care for those people. You have never tried to make yourself understood beyond the level of those who try to learn *your* language; therefore, you don't fit. You will be a foreigner forever. You will have labor problems, you will have government problems, you will always work through interpreters." I don't think that will change by the year 2000. What we're looking for is a world of understanding, and whether we like it or not it's going to have more than one language.

Now, having said that, I would like to hold the coats while the panel discusses whether or not it agrees with Dr. Kirkpatrick that labor unions will be unnecessary and disappear by the year 2000.

DR. HOLLISTER: This question is addressed to the other three panel members.

DR. HENRY: My answer is, no, they will not disappear by the year 2000.

MR. MITCHELL: Will they change?

DR. HENRY: They will change and disappear by the year 2100 provided that management doesn't do something to resuscitate them about the year 2050! The basis for my statement is this: Having spent 100 years developing, these organizations are not going to be eliminated in 33 years, but they may be eliminated in another 100 years. Here are some of the techniques that are going to do it.

As specialized trade unions have developed, membership has become more restricted, specialization narrower, and jurisdictional disputes more common and more bitter. But some farsighted corporations have started programs of multiskill training in which an expert or a journeyman in a given trade union is encouraged to become proficient in another trade. As he becomes proficient in both, he agrees to work in the two trades, and he gets a higher rate of pay than the fellows who can work in only one trade. What has happened in a number of industrial organizations recently is the reintroduction of the old millwright trade which labor unions spent 100 years trying to eliminate. And who are the buyers of this new millwright trade? The labor unions. With the membership's multiple skills, there is no need to wait for the brick mason to come along after the electrician has been here; one man does the work of both and he gets rewarded accordingly. He's a big wheel because he can do more than other people. The result is progress, not phenomenal but steady, over the past 10 or 15 years toward multiskilled affiliations. We're now seeing the millwrights again under new names—plant mechanics, refinery mechanics, shipbuilding mechanics—instead of welders and bricklayers and electricians.

Dr. Hollister: Dr. Bass?

Dr. Bass: All I can do is speculate about several different possibilities. First, some trade unions certainly have become rich enough to buy stock in firms and control them. I say that seriously. I don't see any reason why a union with a large enough fund couldn't buy enough stock, say 1 or 2 percent, to control a fairly large corporation.

Voice: They do now.

Dr. Bass: A second possibility is some unions will gain enough political power in certain areas to control whole communities in a realistic way. They may even take a form whereby they are able to dictate the political setup.

Third, they may, as in Norway, join with management to sponsor research, to promote the well-being of both union and management in a way that leads to the survival and benefit of both. Some experts who have looked at the decline of the labor unions suggest, too, that one area where unions will tend to become more important is the planning and design of new jobs, following in the steps of ILGWU, which worked with the management of the dress industry in the 1930's and 1940's to help to improve efficiency.

Fourth, unions may develop, as has been the trend in Yugoslavia, to where workers' councils elect the management, presumably for four years. The retiring management, as I understand it, doesn't return to the labor force but finds itself new jobs in other companies. The workers thus become the controlling influence. This leads to a lot of problems; which may partly account for why the Yugoslavs have made slow progress economically, but the workers at least seem to be fairly satisfied with this arrangement in many parts of the country.

A fifth area in which union activity may get stronger is the organization of minority groups, formerly unskilled. The farm migrant is an outstanding example of the type of worker who may be completely unionized in the years to come.

Sixth, I foresee more trade unionism among white collar professionals. I was certainly impressed by the way management was promoting unionism among engineers when I visited some of the space technology industries in California a number of years ago. Literally thousands of engineers were working in bull pens under conditions that seemed to me not terribly different from those prevailing among blue collar factory workers. Some of the managers I spoke to commented on how, if they caught engineers standing around the coffee pot, they fired them out of hand. These men whose skills were in short supply were being treated no differently from semiskilled, blue collar workers in autocratically run plants. I couldn't help feeling that the organization of engineers, if it hadn't occurred already in such companies, was about to take place.

Indeed, the gains of blue collar employees have impressed professionals and white collar workers in many areas sufficiently for them to organize. I'm thinking about school teachers, for instance. Here, again, I don't see unionism dying out soon. People who in the past saw themselves as professionals have finally brought themselves to the point where they are willing to deal with their employers through trade unions. I don't think this trend will soon be reversed. Growing numbers of school teachers now see trade unionism, not the professional National Education Association, as the solution for their working problems.

For all these reasons, I think organized labor may experience many different trends, and I'm not at all sure whether these are going to take place at the same time. Some unions will die, and some will prosper in the process.

Mr. Appley: I'd like to submit this reaction to Mr. Kirkpatrick's presentation. He preceded his comment about labor unions with a description of a kind of participative management, prevailing in the year 2000, which would introduce workers more and more into the decisions of management. But just remember this for a moment: It is difficult for a member of a labor union to take on the responsibilities of management decision making and remain a member of labor—a fact that has been proved throughout history.

Whenever the head of a labor movement in England becomes prime minister, he ceases to be a representative of Labor. He quickly senses his position as a responsible executive of the British Empire; he no longer feels obligated to labor alone. When codetermination was introduced in Germany after World War II, when by law every company had to have representation of labor on the board of directors, everyone was appalled—this, it was feared, meant the end of industry. But we of AMA now learn, through our activities in Europe over the past six years, that it is no longer feared. Labor union members, once they become members of the board of directors, are no longer labor—they are now management. They recognize this, and they usually rise to the responsibility.

In Yugoslavia—whenever and wherever you take labor into management decision making—it becomes part of management. I think this is what Kirk meant, and never before in my life have I ever dared interpret what he meant.

DR. KIRKPATRICK: I think Larry Appley has put into clearer words exactly what I was saying. I'm convinced that labor unions will disappear if we have this kind of participation. Of course, if we trend more and more toward bad management in the year 2000, we'll have strong labor unions. That's a different kind of situation altogether.

VOICE FROM AUDIENCE: I think the situation in Germany and the situation in Yugoslavia, from which I've just returned, are somewhat different than what I understood a previous speaker to say. In Germany there are two boards of directors, one of which manages only theoretically. The numbers of managerial and worker members are equally matched, with five representatives of management and five representatives of the trade unions, but there is an important eleventh man—an outsider. Besides, the workers do not run the company. I know from my own experience that the true board of directors represents the shareholders and has no worker representatives. Its members meet privately, and they may do so by law. They consider policy and share the real set of books. Codetermination works in Germany because it stops short of giving labor the voice in management that it wanted.

I would submit that, where you have codetermination, labor has not changed its uniform. It is still militant labor, and I would expect that in the next five or six years it will bare its fangs once again. The unions still play a very active political role. Semantically, of course, you're correct. If a trade union member joins the board of directors, he's a manager—there's no getting away from it. But I don't think he gives up his history. It may be true that when a member of a trade union or a member of the Labor Party becomes prime minister he is at that time no longer a member of labor. But, when his party loses power, he frequently becomes a militant member of the trade union movement once again.

In Yugoslavia, it is a fact that the workers' council has elections and employs management. A manager has the right to accept or not accept a job. He works under contract, and there is now a considerable mobility of managers in Yugoslavia. But there are no trade unions in Yugoslavia. Yugoslavia is a Communist country, and what they call a trade union is a semantic deception. The people who belong to it are not willing members of a trade organization; everybody who works in that factory is a member of the union, like it or not. There are no open shops or closed shops. Those of us who believe in the free enterprise system are pleased by what we see in Yugoslavia because it tends to weaken what is taking place in the Soviet Union. We are attempting to prove, and Yugoslavia helps us to demonstrate, that there is a middle way under Marxism, but the Yugoslavs have nothing that in any way resembles a trade union movement as the term is understood in the West.

I would agree, however, with your interpretation of Dr. Kirkpatrick's remark. We can assume that organized labor in the sense that we have it now will diminish by the year 2000.

Dr. Hollister: We're now coming close to the time when we have to close. I'm going to ask each panel member to take two minutes, and no longer, to sum up what he sees as the high points of our discussion tonight.

DR. BASS: I'd like to take my two minutes to make the observation that we see here something that was started by Dr. Gilbreth and is now ending with the previous speaker: namely, these days we can look on a worldwide basis for new ideas.

An Indian student recently listened to a discussion of Nonlinear Systems, a California company that broke up its assembly lines and introduced the use of small groups to maximize both job satisfaction and production. Afterward, he remarked, "I came to this country to find out about the rationalization of work. Now I'll go back to Papa in India and tell them we've being doing things right for the past 3,000 years."

When I told this story to Norbert Simon, he said, "Yes, but Papa's factory, no doubt, is subsidized by the Indian Government because it's so inefficient." There's a big difference between the feudal system of a chief and his Indian followers and, say, Rensis Likert's notions about group-oriented, group-centered management.

To me, the problem of using this worldwide information we're gathering in the behavioral sciences takes the form of a question. To what extent do the peoples of the world have to move through the rational forms of organization as represented by American industry in the year 1900 before they're ready for the group-oriented approach to management that we think we're pushing toward now in the United States? And to what extent can they skip this phase and move directly from a sometimes feudal world to this new one we're trying to create?

DR. HENRY: In two minutes all I can say is that, on the basis of a number of research projects which have attempted to get at the behavior characteristics of more effective versus less effective managers, we have failed to uncover any differences in racial groups, national groups, socio-economic groups, or any other kinds of groups. Let us quickly add that the sample is somewhat limited, but the same characteristics that are found among successful managers in the United States are also the ones which predominate among successful managers in seven Latin American countries, the four Scandinavian countries, two of the Lowland countries, Libya, Saudi Arabia, and Thailand. If any of you people have companies in other countries and would be willing to offer them as guinea pigs to further elaborate the international sameness of good managers, please let me know.

DR. KIRKPATRICK: I just want to say that there are four big problems in particular which ought to receive a great deal of attention as we move toward this year 2000 and that not one of them has been mentioned here. First, the problem of leisure time as a sociological and economic problem. Second, the development of a science of man that is more specific and at the same time more comprehensive than any that even the behavioral scientists have talked about. Third, alternatives for work and production as basic goals of society. We've put so much stress in our whole society on work. By the year 2000, the problem of scarcity will have passed, the problem of material needs will have passed, and we will have to think in terms of other goals in work and production. And, fourth, man's view of his place in the universe. This is a philosophical and a theological problem that has to be thought about and reformulated between now and the year 2000. It will require more than the superficial attention of the scholar-businessman; rather, it's going to take some scholar-philosophers.

DR. HOLLISTER: It seems to me that, to solve these problems, we're going to have to return to the concept of the dignity and value of labor. We have gotten far away from it and are getting still further away from it under present trends. Somehow, this situation will have to be reversed.

TUESDAY

August 22

Introduction

DON G. MITCHELL
Chairman of the Board, General Time Corporation; and Chairman of the Board, American Management Association

One of the first principles that was taught to me by my mentor, Mr. Appley, was that in the American Management Association we start on time. Whether or not we have any audience is secondary; we go ahead anyway. Over the years, this has allowed me to have a reasonable number of people here when I talk, but my main purpose is to use up enough time so that, when the people on the program talk, they will have an audience. Whether *I* have one is not important.

A second thing that my mentor taught me in the American Management Association is to delegate authority, and so the first thing I'm going to do is delegate the chairmanship of this meeting to somebody else. I'm going to ask my close personal friend and colleague, Mr. Lee Bickmore, president of the National Biscuit Company, to conduct this session.

Mr. Bickmore began his career with Nabisco in 1933 in Pocatello, Idaho. He majored in business administration at Utah State and is also a graduate of the Harvard Business School's Advanced Management Course. Mr. Bickmore is a member of many boards of directors, the Marketing Committee of the National Association of Manufacturers, and the Planning Council of The Presidents Association. In addition, he is a director of the National Industrial Conference Board. Among his many other activities, he is a trustee of Pace Col-

lege in New York City and of the Academy of Food Marketing of St.
Joseph's College in Philadelphia. Finally, he is a fellow of Brandeis
University.

Opening Remarks

LEE S. BICKMORE
President, National Biscuit Company

I'm very happy to be here today. And, because I'm really
overwhelmed with this entire setup, I would like to extend my sin-
cerest congratulations to Mr. Appley, Mr. Mitchell, and their associates for first planning this Center, then constructing it, then so
beautifully decorating this magnificent edifice: a Learning Center
for the man who manages, a noble concept, a motivation, a challenge, an experience, an accomplishment, an involvement. And all of
this in a physical, mental, and spiritual atmosphere that is conducive
to man's greatest growth and development. It is indeed thrilling to
be with you on this occasion.

Our theme—"Management 2000"—is most appropriate. Time
and change are moving so rapidly that now, on the edge of tomorrow, is not too early to start the process of getting ready for 2000.
Yesterday's and last evening's sessions dealt with many basic and
pertinent subjects. Today we have four important topics to cover,
and we're very fortunate that we have four very capable speakers to
handle them.

The first speaker on our program this morning is the distinguished dean of the School of General Studies at Columbia University, Dr. Clarence C. Walton. He will speak to us on the important
subject of "Management in Retrospect." This is a subject with which

he is intimately acquainted as a scholar and as a teacher, as well as through his contacts with management problems in the worlds of business and education. Dr. Walton is a member of the board of Lincoln Life Insurance Company of New York and a trustee of Seton Hall University. He has lectured extensively at important places like IBM, General Electric, and Western Electric, just to name a few. It's a pleasure to have him with us.

Address: "Management in Retrospect"

DR. CLARENCE C. WALTON
Dean of the School of General Studies, Columbia University

When the whole design of this problem reveals so visibly a forward thrust, when men's minds are so palpably concerned with future implications of presently observable changes, and when indeed there is the magic of a year 2000 A.D. to provide dramatic symbolism for an on-rushing future, the invitation to cast a backward glance at management practice and theory induces fears of both futility and frustration for the undertaking. At one time American youth was invited to "go West"—now all men are invited to "go forward."

Substantial evidences of this preoccupation with the future are abundant. In Paris there is a *Futuribles* project, directed by Bertrand de Jouvenel, whose preliminary studies already make fascinating reading; in this country a Commission on the Year 2000 is chaired by a Columbia colleague, Daniel Bell; in England—and with typically characteristic British understatement—there is a Committee on the Next Thirty Years. Even Disneyland abounds with exhibits on our "great big beautiful tomorrows." The list is illustrative and far from exhaustive.

What accounts for this obsession with tomorrow? And is it an entirely new phenomenon? There is little doubt that the rapidity of scientific and technological change has enlarged human sensibilities toward the future; that population explosions force man to consider tomorrow's increases against a declining resource base. But futuristic orientations are not completely novel. In the long-ago time of Greek pre-eminence the ancients, too, were unable to resist the bewitching appeal of a new millennium. Daniel Bell has correctly noted that "men have always been attracted by the mystical lure of the *chilioi,* the Greek word for a thousand from which we get our religious term *chiliasm,* the belief in a coming life free from the imperfections of human existence. Plato, in the Myth of Er which concludes *The Republic,* foretold that departed souls would return to earth after spending a thousand years in the netherworld. And the early Christian expectation of a Parousia . . . placed its hopes for a Second Coming at the end of a thousand-year period. *The millennial point is only thirty-three years away and within the lifetime expectation of more than three-fourths of all Americans now alive."* [1]

But there is a distinctive style in current concerns with the future. If one talks in broad philosophical terms, one can note that Copernicus represented a turning point in speculation. Before him men's eyes gazed toward a future rooted in *space* and not in *time.* The focal point of that future was God, who was somewhere "out there": fixed, immutable, distant. Since Copernicus the emphasis has shifted from fulfillment in space to achievement in time: on changing, immediate, personal experiences. In metaphor, the puppets had revolted and man saw himself as the master of his own destiny.

What is especially relevant here is that Americans sensed almost intuitively what scholars are only now beginning to record. Whereas European peoples thought of a millennium that was far removed, often created and ruled by others, with property shared in common, the American has been obsessed with the notion that he could carve and create a better kind of world in the here and now—the utopia was to be his handiwork, his design, the fruit of his toil, the fulfillment of his vision. And so Americans went to work with a buoyant optimism that enabled them to reconcile almost every kind of paradox.

[1] *Daedalus* (Summer 1967) , p. 640. Author's italics.

Let us consider typical questions posed by philosophers and theologians. What does growth mean: A bigger world or a better one? Americans answered that "bigger was better" and thereby dissolved the chill paradox. Are frontiers always outward in space or inward toward the human personality? The American response was to insist that frontier breaking represented the kind of mobility that made liberty truly operational. Should man want to hit the moon or simply look at it? The American answer: "Both!" And it will likely be realized because few other people are more scientifically venturesome or so incurably romantic.

It is worth continuing to probe the paradox within the framework of business itself. Do businessmen and corporations exist primarily to foster private or public interests? When Arthur Goldberg, in the twilight of his tenure on the Supreme Court, asked a somewhat similar question of an audience of Chicago businessmen, the local newspapers were literally flooded with letters to the editor—not untypical of which was one from a businessman who answered that in our kind of society pursuit of private interests *is* the public good. And so Americans have been able to adapt, in terms of easy reconciliation, historic dilemmas that have made us alternately an envy and a mystery to other peoples.

But has the nation's past in politics and in business become irrelevant to the present and to the future? Are a certain staleness and lackluster the inevitable accompaniments to any excursion into the history of management? What reason, to be concrete, is there in remembering the birthday of a nation whose population then was somewhat less than four million and whose total national output was worth about $1.5 billion in 1967 prices—as contrasted to 200 million Americans today who boast a gross national product of $785 billion? The answer is dramatized most effectively by the sciences themselves. Not long ago, when Morton Nirenberg was given an achievement award by the National Institute of Health, he wrote about the prospects of molecular genetics and asked that man refrain from using the capabilities of programming his own cells "until he has sufficient wisdom to use this knowledge for the benefit of mankind." [2]

This is, in some respects, a startling commentary, for it summons man to slow down the rate of change. History has provided constant examples of the Luddite mentality which sought to impede "prog-

2 *Science* (August 11, 1967), p. 633.

ress," but invariably this was the expression of the "unimportant" and uninformed. Just a half-century ago the very idea, therefore, of convening a body of serious men to ask the following questions would have been regarded as fantastic: How can we *arrest* population growth? Throughout time a rising population has been one of the indexes of a healthy, vibrant, growing society. How can we control certain scientific advances? Historically, every new knowledge and every new invention have been eagerly seized upon and used for people's benefit. How can we channel the rush of men to the city? Their whole past is the story of urban migrations!

Retrospection is relevant because man has wrestled with change before, and the contest provides perspectives.

There are two ways of viewing the past, and each has been exemplified by our two most recent ex-presidents. Dwight Eisenhower repeatedly said that history would produce the final and true verdict of his administration—that is, history would judge and the judges would be men of the future. But John Kennedy carefully read and culled material from inaugural speeches of his predecessors to seek practical guidelines for the vision of a new society. Of the two, the latter approach is more congenial to a group of practical executives who themselves possess power and who therefore point toward a future from the practical perspectives of a past.

The threefold purpose of this brief inquiry may be served if we can (1) identify those germinal or "determinative" ideas which have profoundly influenced the form and content of our political-economic social systems; (2) suggest how these "external" ideas and institutional arrangements have influenced our ideas of business organizations; and (3) pinpoint certain present and visible strains which suggest turning points for the future which may reinforce or transform time-tested concepts.

THE "DETERMINATIVE" CONCEPTS UNDERPINNING THE
SOCIAL SYSTEM

Conceived toward the end of an exciting 18th century, America was the godchild of Europe. But the intellectual backdrop dips further back in time because ideas which truly have the power to move men and to alter institutions move glacially. As the 17th century waned, what was the prevailing political theory? The answer was the "divine right" kingship theory of administration: Rulers were rulers because God made special people for the role. It was simple and effective; so effective, in fact, that from medieval days onward, when barons challenged kings it was never the king himself but rather his evil or inept advisers who were the objects of attack. With the growth of a business class (called derisively the bourgeoisie), men of property were beginning to ask whether God was a really effective political strategist. Or, to put it differently, did Providence have the responsibility for governing? Too many kings appeared so unkingly, whereas many others from the rising social classes who appeared eminently suitable for rulership roles were debarred. It was only a matter of time until the challenge to royal prerogative would come.

Then, too, there was the notion of "status." It was firmly said and widely believed that an aristocracy of blood and of position was the only instrument through which a society could be functionally organized and administered. And yet the thoughtful merchants and derided shopkeepers from the contemptible bourgeoisie were the very people who were painfully aware of the noncontributory nature of the aristocracies that surrounded the thrones of Europe. The ideology was simply not in tune with the times!

The prevailing economic philosophy was mercantilism: What is good for the state is good for the individual. But people were beginning to wonder whether a centralized bureaucracy (with established cartels and monopolies whose sole obligation was to exploit other peoples for the good of the homeland) really added to the wealth of nations. In this kind of setting a new political theory and a new economic rationale were desperately needed.

While the new formulations came from a variety of sources, one could fasten on John Locke and Adam Smith as the prime architects for this new society. Calvin had earlier justified theologically the business *man*. Now we had to have justification for a new political and economic *system*. That was a different kind of intellectual challenge. And how did Locke do it? Wisely he started off in the traditional mold by quoting from the Psalms of David, which told that God's gift of the fruits of the earth made property a community affair. But Locke stepped back to question whether there is anything *not*

owned in common. The answer came quickly—each human being!
And from that, of course, came the notion that if a person added, increased, or substantially enhanced the communality through his own
labors, the fruits of that effort were properly "his." When Locke observed that a deer killed by a certain Indian belonged to that Indian,
and that a fish caught by a certain fisherman belonged to that fisherman, no one denied his logic even though the notion of communal
property and communal possessions had always been stressed in
Christian theology and in descriptions of various utopias.

Now, clearly, one perceives the emergence of a new concept of
private property. Then, from the "property" idea, Locke moved
against divine-right theories to argue that government exists to promote life (which is not a common property) and liberty (which is
the private attribute of that unique life) ; that government should
preserve the liberty of man to carve out his own destiny through his
own labors and through private property. Private utilities become
the common good!

Americans were profoundly influenced by these Lockean notions
and by their author's concept of representative government; namely,
the right to rule by those who had demonstrated a capacity to acquire
property and use it effectively.

So a new political architect had arrived. And then the social structure's theory was completed by Adam Smith with his idea of an exchange economy and a new concept of a profit system to encourage
risk taking. In retrospect, we see that what was created by two men
working in the same intellectual tradition was a completely new notion of property, a new idea for the polity in which the self-interested
search for private good yielded the public weal.

It was in this atmosphere of ideas for representative government,
for fragmented political power to prevent monarchy, in the economic ideas of competition and property, that the American venture
was launched. Note that the American businessman was not called
upon to exercise an imaginative role in creating the structure of the
new society. The theoretical pillars had been well developed for him
by others. The business assignment, therefore, was to work—and this
is important—at the "critical margins" where the theories of property
and of profits, of competition and individual liberty, could be made
operational. To an extent, therefore, the American businessman's

role was circumscribed. He took the broad framework for society as it was. He tended to be politically conservative even when he was most innovative in business. The behavior made sense and is not illogical—as some aver.

TRANSFERRING "POLITICAL" CONCEPTS TO BUSINESS ORGANIZATIONS

It will now be suggested that one of the remarkable developments in American society was the transfer of certain basic "political" ideas to the business structure. We have been so impressed by differences (participatory democracy versus authoritarian "boss" rule in business) that the similarities have escaped attention. To hasten analysis let us accept Peter Drucker's assertion that the corporation is the representative organization of contemporary America and Adolf Berle's conviction that corporate powers may rival those of the sovereign state.

How, then, has the corporation been significantly influenced by the ideas of Locke and Smith? If the corporation is viewed less in terms of its legal structure, less in economic terms as a profit-maximizing entity, and considered in quasi-anthropological perspectives, we see certain concept transfers occurring between the larger society and the corporation. For example, it is evident that the notion of representative government meant people had to be schooled in the idea of accepting the legitimacy of *impersonal* authority. Historically, the very word "sovereignty" meant *personal* loyalty, *feudal* loyalty; people slowly had to learn that one could transfer allegiance from an individual person to an impersonal system.

It is appropriate to recall that when New Englanders faced the wave of immigrants welcomed by business during the late 19th century, they were prone to draw comparisons between themselves and the newcomers. The natives accepted, so it was said, the Roman theory of government which stressed loyalty to the empire; the immigrants carried with them a Byzantine tradition which stressed loyalty to the emperor. It was the impersonality of the "Roman," or Lockean, view that contributed to American acceptance of the corporation. Impersonal government is necessary to the modern corporation. Further, the notions of Adam Smith relating to specialization of labor and specificity of function also were congenial. Heretofore a court physician would attend only the aristocracy; now he would make his skills available in a free market to everyone who could pay, and people would be used where there was a comparative economic advantage. So again we have the idea of the specialized services and distinct functions which were built into the structure of business organizations.

These are, then, the anterior notions which neatly meshed into the formation of the American corporation. Yet, because it was growing to great size, there was a certain ambivalence toward this new instrument. A competitive order rested on small firms. How could the Davids compete with the Goliaths? Notice how, in the beginning, almost every corporation had three powerful limitations imposed upon it—on duration, on amount of capital, and on purpose. By restricting an enterprise to a controlled life cycle, to modest capital, and to one form of production, it was hoped to keep size to manageable proportions.

However, the ideology of small business was to yield slowly but inexorably to acceptance of efficiency based on specialization of function and impersonality of authority. In one sense, the ideology of small business was symbolized by Senator Sherman and the concept of impersonality and specialization by Frederick W. Taylor. And, although scholars quickly identify the Sherman Antitrust Act as the capstone of our belief, the moral fervor which sustained it has subsided while the drive for efficiency has continued to recent days unabated.

It is true that Taylor has been criticized by Drucker and others for being defective in his engineering philosophy because, in fragmenting the job, he wound up fragmenting the worker himself—that is, Taylor allegedly reduced the adult worker to the level of a child. He has been criticized by others on psychological grounds because he divorced planning from doing—which, it is claimed, is alien to human nature. Yet at that particular time (working within the framework of necessary production for profits, for the enhancement of private property) Taylor was summoning us, as he himself said, to a mental and moral revolution. Both manager and worker would later come to understand that it was not simply how to cut the work but how to enlarge the output thereby that was really going to become a major determinant in business.

Concern with the production of goods led perhaps to a neglect of the corporation's role as a social and political unit. When people like Mayo and Roethlisberger and Dickson began in 1935 to take a "human relations" approach to management, they were challenging less the theories of Taylor and more the imported theories of Max Weber. Weber's writing reflects his background as a German sociologist. His experience in the authoritarian German army, his conviction that human nature was fallible and weak, his belief that people were not motivated to work and therefore had to be disciplined, convinced him that bureaucracy was the answer.

These powerful strains led to the formation of an organization based on the presumption that authority always flows from top downward and that, in a conflict between individual and organization, organizational needs must prevail. It was this premise that the human relations theorists challenged. Factors that Max Weber said were beyond human calculus (human emotions, human sentiments, moral judgments) were critically assessed, and the importance of informal organizations was held to be as important to a business organization's success as the older, more formal type of organization based on the scientific management principles of Taylor and the theory of bureaucracy by Weber.

By way of summary, therefore, it may be suggested that Lockean ideas of impersonal authority and Smithian ideas of specialization proved as important in the long-run evolution of corporations as other and better known ideas of market competition and small businesses. The business executive's assignment was to use authority and specialization to meet the enormous material demands of a growing population for essential goods and services; and, in this respect, the American record is unequaled. Now, it may be suggested, the great need is to ask whether—and to what degree—Locke and Smith are relevant to the requirements of the future? And with what consequent changes in organization structure?

VISIBLE TURNING POINTS

It is impossible to do justice to the full range of contemporary developments. In capsule form it is obvious that corporate size is here to stay, that the capacity to produce magnificently has been amply demonstrated, and that the emerging assignment for executives is to use the resources at their disposal in new and different ways. The "human relationists" have demonstrated that the single human being counts, and this, too, is part of the nation's political tradition. This stress on human dignity, which led to due process in the political sphere, is stimulating another transfer of concept into the corporate policies relating to "due process" procedures on dismissal and demotion for middle managers and the white collar class generally. This practice will likely grow.

One could go on to the workforce and speculate still further. Work is one of the firmest contacts with reality, one of the most profound disciplinarians of human effort, and one of the necessary and rich psychological experiences for man. The manager of the future will be deeply concerned with establishing the kind of corporate organization in which the dignity of work will not be lost. A "leisure" society may come, in which the educational and intellectual institutions will probably play a dominant role, but enlargement of work opportunities will remain as a valuable and necessary challenge to business.

What, besides work, is another determinative issue which will face the manager? It is a new concept of property. Clearly, the power of the Federal Government to withdraw or extend franchises, the role of the service state, and the taxing power of government have created a kind of property that now needs re-examination and understanding. Charles Reich of the Yale Law School has said that the old domain of private property, which marked off operationally the limits of personal freedom, has been so eroded that we talk nonsense when we speak of classical and traditional concepts of property. Managers of the future will be called upon to share in the formulation and the operation of a new concept of property in which political power and knowledge will be the most important forms of property.

But if these ideas relate even indirectly to Lockean or Smithian traditions, there is a novel thrust into corporate "social responsibilities" that will require substantial alterations in our heritage. In the past, executives justified their role by pointing out that their responsibility was to produce more goods for more people at competitive prices. They could argue, with Locke, that in mankind's quest for private gains the public good was served. But the existence of urban slums, the ostracism from the workforce of racial minorities, the realities of poisoned air and polluted streams, and the critical state of education combine to force executives to rethink their function and their role.

In this process the Lockean premise is being challenged by an old Aristotelian view that men must *consciously* seek to promote the public good. Rejected is the conviction that the public good is achieved automatically and exclusively through private strivings. Thus self-interest will be enlarged to include the public interest as an imperative in its own right.

Finally, the multinational corporation is also a present reality. The formation of a new kind of international private law to deal with this phenomenon will come, and one can hope that the multinational corporation will serve as a civilizing instrument for the reconciliation of international conflict. Growth by this instrument may make likely the transference of a practice already accepted on the domestic scene: If we now tax citizens of New York to help people in Mississippi, in the future we may have international taxation to help the less fortunate living in Morocco and India and elsewhere. Obviously, business will help shoulder the burden.

The year 2000 A.D. is truthfully tomorrow's margin. Perceptions of that year, dim though they are, lead to the belief that the notions of the dignity of man, the dignity of work, and the dignity of other peoples and other systems will have a powerful impact on the formation of our own society. The insularity that has kept the economy and the polity apart is already breached. The relationship between "goods" and "good" will be increasingly recognized so that similarities and differences being duly noted, businessmen may respond in meta-economic ways to promote a good society.

In the past the business world has had a political and economical system, created by the minds of others, within which to operate. In the future business executives will have an opportunity to participate in the formation of a new, interdependent society. The opportunity can be missed, muffed—or embraced. The historic performance of business provides no clear answer, but it does provide evidence on which an optimistic judgment can be based.

MR. BICKMORE: You know, when we talk about preparing for the year 2000, many of us may think that's a long way off and there isn't much we can do about it. After listening to Dean Walton and hearing about management in retrospect, I'm quite sure now that we're *all* convinced we can't do much about the year 2000. Why? Because what has taken place in the past and what is taking place now already have pretty much dictated what is going to take place in the year 2000. So we should perhaps be very busy assuring ourselves that we're performing our role for the years even beyond 2000.

I couldn't help but speculate about one thing as I listened to Dr. Walton's thesis about the way the world is fast arriving—particularly, we'll say, in the United States, one of the most highly developed countries on the globe—at the point where approximately one-third of our working population is going to supply the goods and services for the entire three-thirds. What, then, will happen to the other two-thirds? What fields of endeavor will they be channeled into? (This ties in with one of last evening's thoughts.) What about this leisure time? And what about the population explosion and the other great problems with which we're confronted now and which will become even more acute in the future? I suspect that the manager in the year 2000 will not be just managing, as we think of it today in the corporate or business sense, but will be managing in terms of all these problems of society. Hence the importance of this conference.

The size and scope of the management problems connected with administering the Budget of the U.S. Government may fairly be said to stagger the imagination. Our next speaker knows more about these problems than anyone else. He is Elmer B. Staats, Comptroller General of the United States. Mr. Staats has spent 26 years in the Federal Government, chiefly with the Bureau of Budgets. He was its deputy director under Presidents Truman, Eisenhower, Kennedy, and Johnson before his appointment as Comptroller General; so he has watched the Federal budget come a long way over the years. This morning, however, he will look ahead and talk to us about government and the manager in 2000 A.D.

Address: "Government and the Manager in the Year 2000"

ELMER B. STAATS
Comptroller General of the United States

The theme of this dedication ceremony is timely and appropriate. It comes by coincidence at almost the midway point between the depression of the 1930's and the turn toward a new century. Who is there that has the perspective to forecast the problems facing the government manager 33 years from today? Viewing in retrospect an equal period of the past, who in or out of government could then have foreseen that

- Nearly 400,000 people would be engaged in a program whose primary objective is a manned lunar landing?
- Primary strategic weaponry would be the Intercontinental ballistic missile?
- Several billion dollars would be committed to provide for a supersonic civilian transport?
- Social Security and Medicare would have been extended to virtually all of our citizens?
- Per capita income—influenced heavily by governmental policies and programs—would have increased from $362 to $2,317?

While the next 33 years may or may not bring equally dramatic and unforeseen roles for government, it is imperative that a government manager understand the basic forces which will determine the problems which he will face in the years ahead. And we may be sure that all government managers will face more problems than they have at any time in the American past.

People may differ as to the variables which will determine both the role of the government manager and the problems that will be facing him in the years ahead, but perhaps they could agree on the following:

- A rapidly growing population, increasingly urban in character. Continued changes in the pattern of family life, with a weakened role for the family unit.
- Rising expectations which grow from an ever increasing standard of living, where expressed needs will continue to outdistance resources and capabilities to meet them.
- An increase in the reliance on the national government for financing and leadership of other governmental programs, with accompanying profound effects upon our Federal system of government.
- A highly intensified struggle to develop and preserve our natural resources and our natural environment which will require additional constraints on exploitation and increased emphasis on scientific research.
- A further blurring of the lines between what is considered public and what is considered private in our national economy.
- And, underlying all of these, the pervasive and unpredictable effect of a rapidly changing industrial technology.

A full discussion of all of these factors is beyond the scope of this presentation. But let me discuss three which now appear to be central to the problems of government management in the years that lie ahead.

This gets me to some extent into the business of making predictions on serious matters which might make hard listening. I will try to couch my remarks in as positive terms as possible. Perhaps you recall the story of a sultan who called a soothsayer and said, "Predict my future." The soothsayer looked at the globe and said, "Sire, I have great news. All your relatives will die before you." The sultan ordered, "Kill that man." Then he called in another soothsayer and said, "Tell me my future." This soothsayer looked into the globe and said, "Sire, I have great news for you. You will outlive all your relatives." And the sultan ordered, "Reward that man." Today's predictions present somewhat the same challenge: We must be sensitive to the choice of words and careful as to their implications.

GROWTH AND URBANIZATION OF THE UNITED STATES POPULATION

Toward the close of Thomas Jefferson's life—in 1825—about 10 percent of our people lived in cities and towns. In 1960 some 70 percent of the population lived in cities and towns—on 1 percent of the land area. The remaining 30 percent lived on 99 percent of the land. By 2000 A.D. 90 percent of the American people will live in urban areas on less than 2 percent of the land, excluding Alaska. One out of ten Americans will live in 19 states containing half our total land, again excluding Alaska. Much of the nation will still be relatively open area.

During the past 30 years perhaps the central forces affecting governmental programs have been these dramatic increases and location shifts of our population. The chief effect of these changes has been the necessity to adjust to mass living in large urban areas. In 1935 the population of the United States was approximately 127 million. We are right now on the point of becoming a nation of 200 million people. In the year 2000—if present trends continue—we may have a population of more than 340 million. The economic and social consequences of our population growth will multiply by geometric progression our responsibilities for providing food and shelter and complicate daily requirements to maintain law and order.

No knowledgeable person should assume that the population of the United States *must* grow to such proportions, but what numbers will it actually reach? Where will the people of the future live? What will be their makeup by race, by education, by residence in and outside central cities or metropolitan areas? Will the future evolve without the problems which we currently associate with the mass migration to the large cities? Or will the slowing of growth—that must come sooner or later—be brought on by pressures generated by the growth itself? The rapid growth of metropolitan areas on the one hand and the depopulation of the rural areas on the other have brought problems in the wake of both developments.

The Rise of Megalopolises. There will be heavy concentrations of people on the Atlantic and Pacific coasts within 50 to 100 miles of the oceans. The population of the Atlantic seaboard today from Boston through Washington is upward of 27 million. Bureau of the Census projections show an increase to over 60 million along this 400-mile strip by 1990. An equally massive metropolitan area is foreseen for the 200-mile Pacific coast zone from Santa Barbara to Los Angeles to San Diego and the Mexican Border.

Herman Kahn, a member of the Commission of the Year 2000 of the American Academy of Arts and Sciences, predicts that by the year 2000 there will be at least three megalopolises in the United States.

> We have labeled these, only half frivolously [he writes], "Boswash," "Chipitts," and "Sansan." Boswash identifies the megalopolis that will extend from Washington to Boston and contain almost one quarter of the American people. . . . Chipitts, centered around the Great Lakes, may stretch from Chicago to Pittsburgh and north to Canada—thereby including Detroit, Toledo, Cleveland, Akron, Buffalo, and Rochester. This megalopolis seems likely to contain more than one eighth of the U.S. population. . . . Sansan, a Pacific megalopolis that will presumably stretch from Santa Barbara . . . to San Diego, should contain more than one sixteenth of the population.[1]

Mr. Kahn foresees that these three megalopolises will contain "roughly one half" of the total United States population, including the overwhelming majority of the most technologically and scientifically advanced and the most prosperous and creative elements. Even Sansan, he notes, will have a larger total income than all but five or six nations.

The Decline of the Counties. Half of the counties of the nation declined in population from 1950 to 1960. But perhaps a more incisive index of metropolitan concentration is the proportion of total national increase that occurred in the metropolitan counties. More than four-fifths of the increase from 1950 to 1960 was in these areas. And the rate of increase for the Negro population in the past three decades has been twice that for the non-Negro population.

Associated with this increase has been the dispersion of population within the central city itself. In the 20 years from 1900 to 1920 the metropolitan population increased 65 percent—75 percent in the central city, 40 percent outside. In the 20 years from 1940 to 1960 the metropolitan population increased 55 percent—27 percent inside the central city, 102 percent outside.

1 Herman Kahn, *Daedalus* (Summer 1967), p. 719.

Accompanying, and contributing to, the expansion in population and urbanization have been spectacular increases in production—on the farm and in the factory, in transportation and communication, and in health and recreation. We have contrived to produce the products required to meet the needs of our society through the skillful application of resourses and inventions and through the liberal use of the raw materials of the world. Today 5 percent of our people grow more than enough food for all the rest.

But to fully understand the portent of these trends, we must go deeper. The recent tragic events in our large cities—although not fully understood—have revealed a certain basic dilemma. This is that, in spite of overall high rates of employment, there has existed in our cities for a generation a group—and some would call it a class —of citizens who have never been fully a part of society as most of us understand it. Here are some of the indications of this problem:

- *Increase in welfare dependency.* Approximately six out of every ten Negro youths reaching 18 have at some time been supported by the Federal Aid to Dependent Children program.
- *Increase in certain types of crime.* For the crimes of burglary, larceny, and auto theft, the Negro rate increased 33 percent between 1960 and 1965. The rates for non-Negroes also increased, but not as much.
- *Missing males in the census count.* At least three years ago we began to realize that the number of Negro males enumerated in the 1960 census was far fewer than it should have been. We now know that altogether the census count missed 10 percent of the Negro population, with a much higher loss rate in young adult males. Something like one male in six had, in effect, simply dropped out of organized society.
- *Educational failure.* For five years or more, we have known that Negro children were doing poorly in the classroom, even in those schools that would have to be described as quite good. For some time we have known the net results: Until recently, about 56 percent of Negro youths called up for the selective service examination have been failing the mental test—a sixth-grade examination.
- *Deterioration of family structure in low-income neighborhoods.* Probably not more than a third of the children of low-

income Negro families now reach 18 having lived all their lives with both their parents. Nearly one-third of the Detroit area Negroes under 18 live in broken homes.

For these people, the overall projections of expected increases in goods and services, better education, urban renewal, better health, and improved science and technology offer little comfort. Ways *must* be developed—indeed, are urgently needed—to provide the substitute for the discipline of the family unit which has played such an important role in our nation's history. In large part, it will eventually be a problem for the government and the government manager.

"CREATIVE FEDERALISM": A GROWING PROBLEM FOR THE GOVERNMENT MANAGER

Ten years ago federal financial assistance to state and local governments amounted to $4 billion a year; five years ago it amounted to $8 billion. It is now running about $15 billion a year and may top $17 billion in fiscal 1968. It is expected to rise to about $60 billion a year by 1975. It is estimated that federal aid will constitute approximately 17 percent of the revenue of state and local governments by 1968.

Estimates of the number of federal aid programs differ. The figure most frequently cited is 170; another estimate puts the number at 220. These programs are financed through 400 or more separate appropriations, administered by 21 federal agencies through 150 major Washington bureaus and over 400 field offices.

Programs are carried on in each of the 50 states. Nearly 92,000 units of local government—each with its own taxing, planning, financing, and operating authorities—are eligible for grants in aid under one or more federal programs.

This seemingly endless number and variety of programs has created perplexing problems. For example, job recruiting can be financed under nine manpower-program sources, adult basic education under ten, prevocational training and skill training under ten, and work experience under five. Funds for on-the-job training can be obtained from five programs; income maintenance is available under nine programs. Eligibility rules, application procedures, allocation formulas, expiration dates, and contracting arrangements vary.

Take the case of a city that wanted to build a river-front park. It found money available under four different federal programs—the open-space program, the outdoor-recreation program, the beautification program, and the parks-development program. Even after making the choice that appeared to offer an advantage, the city was still uncertain as to whether it might have made a better choice.

The Quality of Government. Unsophisticated managers at the local level frequently do not have a sufficiently skilled staff to tackle the maze of differing—sometimes inconsistent—regulations, planning prerequisites, financial matching ratios, reporting requirements, and statistical standards.

This system of seemingly arbitrary organizational patterns and differing legal requirements meshed with local organizations led the President to send a long message to the Congress recently on "the quality of American government." The President took note of the need to "strengthen the federal system through greater communication, consolidation, consistency and coordination . . . to improve the quality of government itself—its machinery, its manpower, its methods."

One proposal aimed at making the federal system more responsive to national needs is to return part of the federal tax revenues to state and local governments with few or no strings attached. Support for this idea is generated by the argument that the Federal Government, through its taxing power, is impairing the capacity of states to raise enough money to take care of their own needs.

The concept of tax sharing is simple, but its application would certainly be highly complex. Even so, an average of one out of every five members of Congress has sponsored or co-sponsored a bill to provide some form of tax sharing. Most of the bills propose a formula under which a percentage of the preceding year's Federal personal income tax revenue would be set aside for tax sharing.

THE SCIENTIFIC REVOLUTION: ITS IMPLICATIONS FOR THE
GOVERNMENT MANAGER

Last year we initiated Medicare in the United States. It coincided with the 100th anniversary of the discovery of antisepsis in surgery. In 1865 Lord Lister, inspired in part by the earlier research of Louis

Pasteur, demonstrated that carbolic acid could be used to free surgical patients from bacteria.

Much of the society we know today is a product of the scientific revolution which is in full tide over much of the world. This is a revolution which has given us modern communications, nuclear power, medical care, increased production of food, and a seemingly limitless number of additional achievements.

In the United States both the number and the proportion of professional manpower made up of scientists, engineers, and technicians are larger than ever before. In 1960 they numbered nearly 2 million; by 1970 they will number 4 million or more. In 1950 the federal budget for research and development was approximately $1.25 billion. By 1967 this had risen to nearly $16 billion—nearly two-thirds of the national expenditures from all sources.

But these figures do not tell the whole story. Without genius, without vigorous and imaginative exploitation of opportunities that scientific insights offered, and without the resolution to apply them to society's purposes, these resources would not have borne fruit.

This is the role of the government manager of the future. It is his job to use his imagination to the limit in order to assure that the benefits of nuclear energy for the civilian economy will not be lost, that the by-products of the space program will be translated into useful applications in other areas, and that patents developed in connection with government contracts will be wholly and freely available to the private economy.

It is the role of the scientist and engineer to discover and develop; it is the role of the manager—be he scientist or engineer, or not—to understand the implications of these developments for both public and private benefit. That is the challenge, as Dr. Jerome B. Weisner, former Science Advisor to the President, said recently. In his words:

> Although most of us appreciate the individual creations of science for what they permit us to do, we do not fully comprehend the fundamental change that the scientific revolution has brought about. . . . Our only hope lies in understanding the forces at work, and then trying to guide the evolutionary process more to our liking.

Dr. Weisner went on to say, in words singularly appropriate to this occasion:

We have seriously unbalanced the learning machine that is our society, and the human aspects of life have not received their share of attention. . . . The fact of the matter is that, until recently, we have not realized the need to grapple with these social problems.[2]

If I were asked what is the central concern of managers today, whether in business, government or educational institutions, or social programs, I would say it is the change in the scale of movements and in the sweep of events. This change of scale goes right across the board from the pace of increase of new inventions to population growth to communications to weaponry.

For the government manager this change in scale means that everything tends to be pushed to Washington faster and faster in bigger and bigger briefcases. All this in turn means that government cannot avoid the influence of crisis in most of its affairs, regardless of whether crisis is immediate or merely potential. It need not be a case of either war or acute economic depression, although this is the way we normally think of crisis. For example:

- So fragile is the texture of peace that the combined forces of Asiatic and African nationalism or the assimilation of nuclear weapons into the status of conventional arms could lead to catastrophic results.
- So sensitive is our economic mechanism that even mild dynamics in the international dollar balance or in the domestic demand-supply relationship can precipitate acute stresses.
- So rapid is the world's rate of population growth that the extreme contrasts between the "have" and "have not" societies can generate dangerous coalitions of political unrest and adventure.
- So intense are our domestic problems of urbanization, education, transportation, aging, and shortages of some types of manpower that we cannot indefinitely make these priorities wait simply because the budget is saddled so heavily with programs that were meant to deal with yesterday's priorities. For today individuals and groups demand action. They refuse to sit and accept their fate.

Our future will turn on reassessing and redefining national priorities. The manager will increasingly live in an economy of priorities

[2] Dr. Jerome B. Wiesner, *The Challenge of Technology*, National Industrial Conference Board, 1967, pp. 4–8.

and of agonizing choices between public purposes and private prefer-
ences. Unless some step is taken toward the achievement of a national
consensus as to our paramount purposes and goals, unless some great
revision comes to pass in the present distribution of revenue sources
among federal, state, and local governments, the crisis of priorities
will be one of the deepest tests of our policy machinery. As such it
will inevitably involve the government manager.

In planning for the future, the manager will have the advantage
of—and must know the value of using—the new technique, most frequently called systems analysis or systems planning, which uses cost
effectiveness as a major ingredient. Thus the decision maker will
have a clearer idea of the choices open to him and the ways of mea-
suring results against planned objectives.

Qualities Government Managers Will Need. These are but a few
random evidences of present and prospective crises. What do they
signify for the kind of government manager needed in the future?
Fundamentally they call for the cultivation of a new attitude of mind
which puts a higher and more consistent value on what might be
termed "anticipation." To do this, we must create within ourselves
the desire to find time in our schedule to think. Tomorrow's executive must not only capably handle the traffic of administration, but
must also see to it that his policy machinery stays several lengths in
front of next year's problems.

Granted that government will from time to time have no escape
from the improvised solution in a given set of circumstances, it simply will not do to fall back consistently upon makeshift answers to
deep and pervading problems. The crash program is usually a pallia-
tive, both expensive and wasteful of talent and resources. It seldom
turns out to the credit of those who launched it. What we want is
answers without excessive reliance on the panic button. There is a
difference between crisis government and crisis administration.

The government manager of the future must have the qualities
of restlessness, of curiosity, of dissatisfaction. This is where administration both supplies and finds its drive and where it makes its contribution to the everlasting process of perfecting the imperfect structure of compromises that we call modern society. The issue is really
the rate at which this incremental process will go on or how strong
the vein of creativity will be in this group we choose to call "management."

If not every manager has it in him to be creative, he still has the opportunity to spread the contagion of leadership down and through the organization so that the environment encourages creativity among those who have the potential. This means less reliance on scripture writing and less emphasis on manuals of procedure, on dogmas of system and method, on the fetish for hair splitting in rubrics of budgeting, personnel management, and methodology, without losing the contributions of these essential disciplines.

If creativity means anything, we have to send our minds beyond the things about which we already feel certain. We have to unleash our notions, our curiosity, our instinct to experiment. It means that we have to break out of our limited mental environment. We have to find out what the other fellow is thinking about and why he's thinking about it. It means rediscovering the fact that there is a convergence somewhere along the line among the various threads of public policy—between science and foreign relations, between housing and health, between transportation and defense, between budgeting and economics.

Contracts, Grants, Regional Compacts. The manager of the future will find himself carrying out more and more public policy through contracts, grants, regional compacts, institutes, foundations, and self-contained business enterprises. This will make management at one and the same time both possible and difficult. The line between public administration and private participation will be less clear than ever, while the hybrid will flourish. And it is here that the manager will have his work cut out for him—in maintaining the essential responsibility that belongs with government, in understanding the fine difference between supervision and interference, and in judging how well the ends of public policy are being served.

It is doubtful that the government executive of the future can be grown and trained exclusively in the career civil service. He will have to have some first-hand experience with unfamiliar environments: the university environment, the regional environment, the business and research environment. We will have to develop an exchange of persons between government and these allied communities through reciprocal internships and residencies. From this there is no escape.

Still another determinant with which we must cope in the coming years is the growing appetite for data—the passion for facts, for information, for probability. This is inevitable as a society draws closer together, as public purposes fuse, as the public and private economies meld, as decision making takes place in a continuum. In this process, the nature of government will resemble less and less a laboratory and more and more the pharmacy, since the medicines we will use must increasingly depend upon accurate prescription.

We will discover, I believe, that law and administration will necessarily seek a precision that they lack today. This will require an understanding of the dynamics of both society and technology that, as I mentioned, we now do not have. Today we seem to be investigating technology to a degree that far outstrips our organized curiosity about society. The collection of refined data, their tabulation, analysis and re-analysis, and interpretation, will be one of government's major occupations, a situation to which we will be driven if we do not seek it voluntarily. And the reason is that government is the only unselfish convenience we have for conducting such an enterprise.

Perhaps the most important and the least understood development in the new technology is the revolution in information—the continuing increase in the speed, capacity, and versatility of big computers and long-distance communication facilities; the rapidly proliferating uses of electronic storage, retrieval, and processing of information. The big computers will soon be joined together in nationwide and even worldwide networks, and before very long they will have outlets in every office and home. This could result in the elimination of books and banks, the disappearance of printers and stenographers, and a revolution in newspapers—as television programs have already shown us.

The manager of the future must have a comprehension of the values and limitations inherent in the use of data, the art of timing in data collection, the process of designing the structure of investigation, the ethics of reporting and disclosure, and the fine judgment that interprets the significance of the information and applies it to policy making. Why? Because the manager will have to rely more on the top of his head than, as in the past, on the seat of his pants. He will have to be at home with theoretical statistics and the rarer altitudes of mathematical science.

The Meaning of Science and Technology. The manager of the future must grasp the importance of science and technology in the relations between government and all the rest of society. World wars may have produced the environment which gave science and technology the spark they were waiting for; but science and politics—both national and international—now go together, and neither can function without the other. That is the central fact of our time, and it can only have one meaning for the future.

The manager of the future must realize that science and technology will continue their penetration of every facet of public policy and public management. For the executive this means that we must close the gap between the two cultures, as C. P. Snow describes them, the scientific and the humanistic. We can no more leave science to the scientists than we can leave government to the politicians. We must comprehend the scientific environment; we must find ways to make science and public policy compatible, not merely as to national purpose, but particularly as to a working compatibility.

The problems of administration are surely destined to require this kind of understanding of science and technology. How else shall we make a contribution to solving the difficult problems of weapons control and disarmament, eliminating air and water pollution, harnessing our energy sources for both human and industrial needs, understanding the requirements of education and vocational motivation, meeting the requirements of an exploding population at home and abroad, providing the rising nations of the world with gifts of technology since our material resources will not be sufficient to share with them?

No problem is more directly related to the future of our democratic society than the problem of attracting the best talent to public service. While a democratic society's government is not expected to have a monopoly of the ablest people produced by that society, neither can it afford to provide for the public service an iota less than its full share of the talent available. The reason has been succinctly stated by the late Clarence B. Randall:

> The ultimate effectiveness of our governmental process, whether in Washington, or in the state capitals, or in the city halls, rests squarely upon the quality of the career officers, the permanent civil service.

In the past the consequences of an average or below-par public service have not been nearly as serious as they are now. As the role of government grows, and as the decisions of public officials at all levels of government have a more and more direct effect both on our daily affairs and on our prospects for the future, the quality of our public service becomes a major public concern. In the words of Mr. Randall:

> Today, as never before, the administration of our government calls for excellence in leadership. We need thoroughly competent executives, acquainted with the most modern techniques in managing large enterprises, from cost accounting to good human relations, from sound staff work to automatic data processing. We need scientists in our race for pre-eminence in all fields of research. Above all we need a continuing source of replenishment of this talent.[3]

Importance of Staff Training and Development. We in the General Accounting Office, for example, recognize the importance of training and staff development. We have provided a full academic year of special or advanced training at the university level or its equivalent for about a hundred of our people in the past six years. We are giving particular attention to the adaption of the computer to government planning and programming, systems analysis, and cost effectiveness.

I would emphasize particularly in staff development work the need to focus on the initiative shown by each individual. Without this no training investment is worth the cost. An individual's own efforts and interest (aside from his ability) must be the primary test as to whether the training program can be justified.

CONCLUSION

The meaning of what I have been trying to say today is nowhere better expressed than by the Secretary of Health, Education, and Welfare, Mr. John W. Gardner. Here are his words from a commencement address this year:

> We now know beyond all doubt that nations die from within, and they are attacked less often by traitors within the gate than by traitors within the heart—complacency, apathy, cynicism, tolerance, self-deception, and an unwillingness on the part of the individual to lend himself to any worthy common purpose.

3 Clarence B. Randall, *A Businessman Looks at Government Pay*, a public service report of the National Civil Service League, 1962, 15 pp.

H. G. Wells wrote in 1906 that Americans were addicted to "a sort of optimistic fatalism." He was saying that Americans looked upon difficulties and challenges as opportunities and not as obstacles. This healthy philosophy is in sharp contrast to statements heard too frequently today. One nuclear physicist recently defined an optimist as "someone who still believes the future is uncertain."

The responsible citizen is one who is willing to admit that he does not comprehend the future in this dangerous era, yet knows he is called upon to deal with and solve what he may not fully understand. We can join, perhaps, with Charles Dickens in his more balanced, although seemingly paradoxical, opening lines of *A Tale of Two Cities*:

> It was the best of times, it was the worst of times, it was the age of wisdom, it was the age of foolishness; it was the epoch of belief, it was the epoch of incredulity; it was the season of light, it was the season of darkness; it was the spring of hope, it was the winter of despair.

More apropos is a statement in a recent article by Elting Morison in the *New York Times Magazine*:

> How to give individual men the evidence they need to make sensible judgments about the kind of world they want to live in and how to give them the power to make their judgments stick, that is the unfinished business of the next third of the century.[4]

This statement applies particularly to the governmental manager of the future.

MR. BICKMORE: I'm sure we're all well aware of the fact that government plays an important role in our lives today and that, undoubtedly, it will play a much more important role in our lives in the future. I was impressed, Mr. Staats, with your thoughts about the scale of the coming changes, the bigness of the concept, and with your comment that the gap between the "have" and the "have not" peoples seems to be getting wider. It would appear, therefore, that we have a problem in the selection of crises as priorities. Which seems to me to tie in with the teaching of AMA that, once we get all the data which scientific developments have made available to us, the judg-

4 Elting Morison, *The New York Times Magazine*, Vol. VI, April 24, 1966, p. 34.

mental factor becomes even more important. The manager, through his experience, knowledge, and intuition, must still make timely decisions on some very vital matters.

I was interested, too, in your thoughts on how you're going to get qualified managers in government. I'm sure you have the same problems there that exist in business, education, and other areas of our society.

Finally, I was intrigued with the H. G. Wells statement, in 1906, that we Americans are given to "optimistic fatalism" and the possibility that our philosophy and outlook may be changing today. This probably raises the sort of question that is sometimes heard. Is opportunity a thing of the past? Has America reached its peak and begun to go over the hill? Here is something that we can well contemplate.

Opening Remarks

LEE S. BICKMORE
President, National Biscuit Company

We had a wonderful session this morning. We were treated to some real professional information, talent, and mental gymnastics. It is wonderful to exercise our thinking powers and attempt to get things in the right perspective; to see exactly where we've been and where it appears we are going.

What kind of man will be in the forefront of management leadership in the year 2000 A.D.? If anyone knows the answer to this question, it is our next speaker: Mr. Frank J. Nunlist, chairman of the board and chief executive officer of the Worthington Corporation.

Mr. Nunlist's background is in chemical engineering and corporate management. He is a director and member of the Executive Committee of the American Management Association; he is also a director of the Market Research Corporation of America, Alco Products Incorporated, and Electric Machinery Manufacturing Company.

Mr. Nunlist is no stranger to noncorporate management; he is a member of the Citizens Committee for Higher Education in New Jersey, the Greater Newark Development Council, and the Greater Newark Hospital Development Committee. I know he will have some fascinating insights to offer on management leadership in the year 2000.

Address: "Management Leadership in the Year 2000"

FRANK J. NUNLIST
*Chairman of the Board and Chief Executive Officer,
Worthington Corporation*

Two-thirds of the 20th century has passed. Immediately ahead lies the last third of the last century of the second millennium since Christ. We live in a world of violence and turmoil. Wars, thankfully relatively small ones, break out around the world. There are threats and outbreaks in the Congo, in the Middle East, in Vietnam, on the Chinese-Indian border, in Hong Kong. Crime and violence run rampant on our streets at home. College campuses around the world are in revolt.

This is indeed a time to take stock of our world and its society and to determine, if we can, what approaches, what attitudes, and what means a new leadership must take if we are to move people toward the goals for which they were truly destined. This last third of this century may mark a turning point in the affairs of man. I believe, in fact, that it will—providing men of goodwill determine that this be so. I believe that we stand on the threshold of a new renaissance in the affairs of man. I believe that we are about to exchange will for idea in the world. I believe that the fulcrum will shift from power to persuasion, from physical force to creative intelligence.

It is a time to find out why our leadership has failed to produce better understanding, better results both domestically and internationally, and more rapid progress toward man's God-given right to life, liberty, and the pursuit of happiness. To do this, I believe it is necessary to review the patterns of history. This will also help us in projecting the patterns of the future. As much as we should like to engage in crystal-ball gazing, in the art of prophecy, I cannot but feel that changes in our society and its leadership will develop only as our society is prepared to accept change.

So let us look back briefly. Sixty-seven years ago, at the beginning of this century, the United States had just emerged from the first war which began to establish it as a leader in the community of nations. Those portions of the world which were industrialized were just emerging into the full flower and fruits of the Industrial Revolution. The automobile was new. The press was talking of big business, big railroads, and big banks; of mergers; and of monopolies. Much to the dismay of management, trade unions were beginning to emerge as a potent force on the business scene. And we were faced with the tragic problems of unemployment, hunger, closed banks, and near-panics. Later in the first third of our century a large portion of the civilized world was engaged in a major world war.

Thirty-three years ago we were in the midst of a great depression, a depression felt most by those of us here in America, but a depression that in fact enveloped the entire world. There were marches on the White House, there were breadlines, there were shanty towns, and there was turmoil. And perhaps for the first time in man's history society began to look to the great benevolent and paternalistic government for solutions to the problems that existed. Again, at about the midpoint of the second third of our century, much of the world was involved in another world war. Must we look forward to another in the last third of our century?

It seems to me, looking at history in another light, that this century has been roughly characterized by three periods of industrial development. In 1900 we were emerging from a human-muscle method to mechanical methods of producing goods. By 1933 human power had largely been supplanted by horsepower, and we began emerging into a technological society which supplemented mechanical power with brainpower. Now, as we face the last third of the century, it appears to me that we are emerging into a period of sociological power, which perhaps will be the most marvelous of all; for, if we are skilled in our leadership, this period will use industrial muscles and technological brains as leverage to move us ahead socially.

As we trace leadership through the ages, names like Alexander the Great, Julius Caesar, Napoleon, Disraeli, George Washington, Hitler, and Churchill come to mind. It is to be noted that as we hastily construct this list of leaders we tend to include primarily the names of men of conquest. In the business world, too, past leaders' names that come quickly to mind are Morgan, Kreuger, Vanderbilt, Gould—men whose influence rested on naked economic power. We seldom reflect on the leadership associated with such names as Aristotle, Plato, Marcus Aurelius, Aquinas, Locke, Kant, Schopenhauer, Jefferson, or Dewey. We must not overlook the contribution the philosophers have made, but they have only created the ideology which has been used as an excuse for conquest by power-structure leaders. Historically, idea leadership has been only a secondary force.

As we contemplate the history of political leadership, which has largely stemmed from military power, we need to recognize the growth of the frightful implements of destruction which were the basis of this power. From the bow and arrow, the spear, and the mace we have progressed to gunpowder, to rifles, cannon, tanks, aircraft, rocketry, and nuclear armament. I suggest to you on this August 22, 1967, that we are on the threshold of an era when the awesome power of destruction has been so perfected that it no longer is acceptable as a springboard for leadership. Just as the enforced leadership of unbridled economic power reached such extremes that the public and the government rejected it—mitigating it with antitrust laws, regulatory agencies, and that great equalizer, the income tax—so, too, will leadership based on military destructive power be curbed. Social and philosophic considerations no longer can accept a leadership based on power. Instead, we are awaiting anxiously a leadership based on the *abandonment* of power.

Although in over 2,000 years we have moved from a purely agrarian society, through feudalism, into a world of industrial production, military might during each period has been predominant. Now I suggest to you that we are on the doorstep of a new society, with new challenges and new kinds of horizons to explore. For all these centuries mankind could not be expected to think clearly about the development of ideas in his civilization. Man was forced by need to preoccupy himself with acquiring the bare necessities of life, and his instruments for acquiring the necessities were war and conquest. This is no longer true in our country, nor in most of the industrialized nations of the world. Nor will it be true in the year 2000. I am convinced that affluent mankind is shouldering its responsibility to upgrade the lot of marginal peoples, if for no other reason than the selfish reason of protecting its own affluence.

It is not incredible, then, to suggest that we may be moving from a leadership through conquest to a leadership through ideas. It is not incredible to believe that we may soon accept Plato's thought that only when the kings and princes of the world have the spirit and power of philosophy will justice prevail. In order to examine the pattern of leadership that will be required in the year 2000, it is necessary to examine the basic assumptions we make about the world as it will be in the year 2000.

I believe that, with the growth of the total economy of the world, free enterprise will probably be somewhat more regulated than it now is. On the other hand, I am equally inclined to believe that the totalitarian economies of the world will enjoy a great deal more freedom than they now do. I am sure that we will be faced with new methods of credit and monetary arrangements to facilitate the exchange of wealth between the "haves" and the "have nots" of our world. In fact, the free-trade world will probably exist by the year 2000.

Retirement age in the industrial nations surely will advance to 55 and perhaps to 50, thus confining useful working careers to 25 or not more than 30 years. Yet, in those 30 working years, an individual will be able to provide for the sustenance of a life expectancy of perhaps 90 years. With this change alone each individual will have at least 20 to 25 years more of his lifetime available for self-improvement, for broadened education, and for contribution to the welfare of society as a whole. Although Herman Kahn, director of the Hudson Institute, has said that the amount of leisure available to Americans by 2000 could be catastrophic, I don't believe it will prove to be so. Man will not spend all this new time in pursuit of recreation—lazing in the sun, climbing to the mountaintops, traveling to foreign climes. It is our nature to want to serve usefully. Therefore, we will inevitably broaden our interest in the social sciences, in the development of the arts, in the cultivation of the mind and soul.

For more than a century the world has been engaged in the process of increasing man's output by placing mechanical muscle at his command. Perhaps one of the key economic problems of the advancing nations is the fact that they can now produce more things than they can use and the markets for these products are limited. This necessarily will require more consideration as to the distribution of this excess production, either to benefit nations less fortunate than we or to ultimately free all of mankind from the slavish burden imposed in the Garden of Eden.

In the last few years we have begun to extend the powers of the minds of men through the use of electronic data processing, electronic communication, electronic entertainment, and a whole host of new techniques. As we increase man's mental capacity through the use of devices that will do his routine thinking chores, we will accelerate our technical abilities at an even faster rate.

Some people with long memories coupled with readings from the history books of the early years of this century appear to feel that businessmen and business leaders have not been changing quite as rapidly as the accelerated change in our environment. Money grubbing, greed for power, and a concern for his own selfish welfare often are the traits attributed to the businessman. Yet business leaders and their organizations actually have been rapidly adjusting to the new environment. The time has arrived, I suggest, when our technology must increasingly be managed for the sake of the social good. We must begin to reason from the particular to the general. In this process, we will have to recognize that our induction may not be as precise, as valid, as completely correct as the technology itself. We will be looking outward from our businesses to the rest of the community, from our community to our state, from our state to our nation, and further outward to other nations. The inevitable balance wheel will have to be a policy-making government structure.

The public has demanded that it be considered as important in the operating of our economy as business itself, and it has enforced its demand through an ever-growing, government-controlled regulatory system. Businessmen have increasingly found themselves in conflict with the aims of government, or perhaps more realistically in conflict with the aims of the nonbusiness community—with the public at large. And as this has occurred, particularly since the end of World War II, enlightenment has begun to appear on the scene with increasing radiance. Businessmen today recognize the need for concern about the communities in which they operate. They recognize the need for concern for the public weal. They recognize the need for concern for their employees. They recognize the need for concern for the long-range direction of our society. With recognition have come the forces which are developing a business leadership of social relevance, one that looks outward at the world in which it operates.

Businessmen have had to be increasingly more interested in the government and its operations than they have been classically. Does not all of this, therefore, suggest the necessity for training the new breed of leadership and in particular the new breed of business leadership that will have its basis in ideas? And the ideas themselves must change, for they will be, not merely technical in scope, but rather broad-gauged and philosophic. The need for a leadership in which ideas and intellectual force will replace the power and the strength of mere machinery, of mere armament, of mere lust for power and greed and selfishness is clear. Will selflessness not replace selfishness in the leadership of tomorrow?

The year 2000 seems a long way ahead to you and to me. Yet it is only 33 years from now. The young man who graduates from college this year will, in the year 2000, be about my own present age. This young man's challenge, his need for knowledge, his ability to achieve personal satisfaction will be far greater and far more complex than we can now visualize. And this young man 33 years hence is going to have to lead an entirely different following from that we know today. He will need to be a leader among men whose needs to satisfy their hunger and keep themselves and their families clothed and sheltered will no longer predominate. He will lead men whose desires move in a variety of directions. The needs of the young and the needs of those who have retired are quite different from the needs of those who work. In his first 30 years the manager of the future will be maturing through a variety of processes. For his second 30 years he will be leading the improvement in standards of living, after which he will emerge into a world of security for himself with a desire to help others become equally secure.

From these inevitable changes in man's expenditure of his time and energy will come, I believe, a greater desire for individualism as people flee from the protective mantle of mass production, mass marketing, and mass identification. I suggest to you, therefore, that George Orwell may not have been accurate when he projected a leadership by Big Brother for a faceless society. I believe that the characteristics of our society will be far more varied than they are today and that Big Brother and Big Father will not be wanted or accepted.

What will be wanted will be thoughtful, creative, imaginative, understanding, intelligent leadership—leadership that will be effective because its reasoning toward the common weal is valid, sound, and thoughtfully conceived; leadership that shuns the use of power, manipulation, and fear. There is no doubt in my mind that leadership by thought will replace leadership gained through the power of money, the power of politics, the power of military might, or the power of personality.

The engineers, the scientists, the mathematicians will continue to be needed as problems develop in our congested society. Increasingly, however, the real leader will have a broad education and background. The social sciences will play an important role in resolving the problems of a society with more leisure for thought, culture, and individualism. Our future leader, constantly adding to his education, will have a varied business background rather than a background in a specialized field. His thinking processes will tend to be inductive rather than deductive.

The leadership of force will be replaced by a leadership of persuasion, a leadership that truly implements McGregor's Theory Y—which holds that men who are working respond more to persuasion, to liberty, and to ideas than to supervision and to fear. He will be a leader who activates people with ideas instead of propelling them with force. This new leader, while perhaps originally trained in a technical specialty, will, through further training and broad experience, have become a social-minded generalist. He will no longer lead by looking inward at his own organization as segregated from the environment in which it exists. Rather, he will look outward as well with concern for the environment in which his company lives and for the public which it serves. This business leader of the future must be the single centripetal force that balances the interests of customer, employee, investor, and the public.

That's quite a prescription for any man to fill if he is going to be a leader 30 years hence. We must focus on training him, broadening him, and developing him now. Remember that at my present age he will either have retired four years ago or be planning his retirement party next year. If we assume that his formal education ends at age 22, he has only about 18 years in which to gain the knowledge and experience to fit him for a leadership role that will last little more than a decade.

The leader of the year 2000 will be a very young man. His goals will be broad and his influence great. He will reason from the particular to the general and will look outward at the conflict of forces to see that they are kept in balance and in proper perspective. He will realize the great strengths that lie in the point and counterpoint of individualism. He will spend more time in creating satisfactions for people as individuals and will tend to destroy some of our present concepts of mass management. He will understand that man is neither a machine nor a physical animal, but is endowed with creative intelligence, creative drive, and the will for good, not merely the insensate will to live.

MR. BICKMORE: Thank you very much, Frank, for real gems of knowledge with respect to the manager in the year 2000. I couldn't help but think, when you were talking, of a statement that was made by Dr. Philip Lodge, the great Harvard professor. He said something like this: "You lose your leadership only when you cease to lead." And, while we're talking about the leadership job of the manager in the year 2000, I think that probably between now and then, in preparing people for leadership, we're going to have to be very sure that we in the business community do not lose the lead."

I thought your prediction that we will change wealth for ideas was very interesting. In other words, whereas in the past wealth has been the thing that has seemed to get us power and prestige or influence, in the future it will be ideas. We are emerging into a period of sociological power. For all of us who have been schooled in the university of profit and loss, I suspect, it is going to be a little difficult to make the adjustment—to begin to look at things from this sociological standpoint. Yet, as you pointed out, Frank, we're going to extend the power of the mind so that it can comprehend these things, so that we can throw out the past and look at the future and even the present from a much broader point of view. We will move from the specific to the general.

I also enjoyed your statement that the businessman, instead of looking inward into his business, as we have all been doing almost with blinders on, in the future will be looking outward to the world about him—which will give him a chance to find his particular place in it and learn what he should do to carry his share of the work and make his contribution to overall goals.

You said that instead of leading by force the young managers of the future will lead by persuasion; that their subordinates will not respond out of fear as they have probably done in the past. Then the thought struck me that action based on fear is the very antithesis of intelligent action. And, therefore, by getting the necessary knowledge and preparing ourselves to leading intelligently, we are, of course, insuring that the action will be that much better.

Frank, I know that your practical experience and your knowledge of this subject has made possible a real contribution to all of us here this morning.

Our next speaker is Dr. Herbert E. Longenecker. Mr. Nunlist has told us about the quality of leadership we will need in the year 2000 to manage the affairs of this nation. Clearly, to prepare young men and young women for the task that management poses is going to be a profound challenge to the educational establishment of the United States. Dr. Longenecker, president of Tulane University, will tell us something about how our colleges and universities plan to meet this challenge.

Dr. Longenecker has had a most distinguished career in education. He has held two deanships and been a member of the faculty at the University of Pittsburgh, and he was vice president of the University of Illinois before assuming his present position. In addition, he is adviser, board member, and chairman of a host of councils and committees in the fields of education, government, and industry. If anyone can enlighten us about educational preparation for the manager of the year 2000, it is Dr. Herbert E. Longenecker.

Address: "Educational Preparation for the Manager in 2000"

DR. HERBERT E. LONGENECKER
President, Tulane University

I wish I could agree that I have the presence of mind to accomplish the task set for me. Frankly, one approaches an assignment like this with the humility that our first speaker this morning commented on. Really, we are here simply because of the persuasiveness of one man, Larry Appley. He has the ability to command a presence, if not a performance. When Larry asks you to undertake a task, you accept. And, when he combines an occasion such as this with the group of distinguished people who are here, both on the program and in the audience, one does feel very humble at having the privilege of the platform for a few minutes.

I am reminded of a story that a man who was visiting Tulane University gave us last year. He was a diplomat-in-residence who had had experience in Russia during his Foreign Service career. There, he had picked up a choice anecdote that seems apropos.

This story is about a Russian muzhik who was trudging home over the cold tundra one day when he spied a little bird obviously in difficulty and just about to expire. Being a very kind-hearted man, he took off his big gloves, reached down, picked up the little bird, and held it in his hands to warm it and restore some semblance of life. But he wasn't doing very well until a big brown cow came along and deposited a large steaming dropping. Now, being a very intelligent as well as kind-hearted man, the muzhik knew exactly what to do. He immersed the little bird up to its neck in the dropping, and in a few

moments the warmth had revived the bird. It was singing happily as
the muzhik went on down the road to his home. A few moments later
another muzhik came along who was also very kind-hearted but not
quite so intelligent. Seeing the little bird immersed in the dropping,
he reached in, took it out, and placed it gently on the barren, cold
tundra where it promptly expired.

The Russians have a moral for this story. It runs something like
this: "He who puts you into it is not necessarily your enemy." A second moral is: "He who takes you out of it is not necessarily your
friend." And, most importantly, a third moral is: "If you're in it,
don't sing!"

Down in the country where I've moved, there are Cajun stories.
One I like is about a Cajun oil-well driller whose point of view was
that, if you can't strike oil within ten minutes, stop borinig! I intend
to follow his advice.

The prescription given to us this morning is one which I would
have welcomed having in detail prior to standing before you and
commenting on education for the manager in the year 2000. Failing
that, I had to make some assumptions, just as Frank did a moment
ago. But I think, for the most part, the assumptions I've made are
very much the same as his.

First of all, I'm not sure exactly whom we mean when we talk
about the "manager in the year 2000." Perhaps we mean a man of 50
at that time. If so, he's 17 years old right now and next year he'll be
entering college. Is this the person we're talking about? Very probably.

Or are we talking about the man of 40 who's just started elementary school? Or the man just being born this year? In the latter case,
we need to think about preschool education as well as elementary
and secondary education, followed by the college world and all the related experiences that come from outside the formal patterns of our
educational setting.

What is important for us to emphasize at this point, if we're
really talking about the manager of the year 2000, is that we have a
job to do *right now*. And we've got to get on with that job, whether
we know exactly how to go about it or not.

By the year 2000, the wisdom that will have been accumulated
in this Manager Learning Center, plus the effectiveness of its programs, will undoubtedly have improved the quality of manage-

ment in both the private and the public sector. We can, of course, anticipate that the task of management will continue to present some rather severe difficulties—intense competition, fickle customers, unreasonable labor, complex and perhaps even absurd governmental regulations, and so on. But, in spite of these problems, the manager will be expected to operate successful programs in business and industry—that is, at a profit which will be adequate enough to attract continuing investment of capital for regeneration and growth. However, even this will not suffice, as has been amply demonstrated here this morning.

In our society, it is unlikely that the successful corporation of the future will be free of harassment, operating in the absence of public belief that its power is being used for public benefit. Part of the manager's problem will therefore be the creation of a favorable attitude toward the corporation—a process which is already under way and will be accentuated, as I see it, during the remaining years of this century.

Against this background, what are we thinking about in terms of education for the manager in the year 2000? Basically, I think we have it well laid out. My task this morning may be simply to summarize some of the things that have already been said.

For example, in the opening remarks today we heard a brilliant presentation based upon reflections. What was it, actually? It was a look at the heritage of the past, a distillation of some of the really important things that have counted in terms of man's understanding of ideas, man's understanding of people, man's understanding of organizations, and the interactions and interrelationships that must exist to bring these together in a meaningful way in order that action may result.

If we're truly to understand our heritage, we must ask: Can we do it just by a series of rote experiences in learning? Can we understand where we've come from, who we are, what tortuous paths brought us to this present point, simply on that basis of rote learning?

If we are to achieve the kind of objective I would like to see us set for the manager in the year 2000, I expect that we will need to find faculties and develop new approaches in our educational system which will enable us to raise the level of excitement for a larger number of our total students. Specifically, I wonder what the factors were that, entering into Dean Walton's educational preparation, enabled him to reach easily and with such obvious facility into the rich heritage of the past in such a fashion as to be able to construct and synthesize a totality of experience in just a few moments. It's that kind of rich experience and that kind of human understanding which I believe the manager of the year 2000 will have to develop as a basic background for his readiness to accept the responsibilities of that day, 33 years from now.

Certainly he must understand, also, the nature and main directions of change in the world environment. Unless the manager of the year 2000 has some live connection with that changing setting in international affairs, I believe he will not be as well prepared as he should be.

Then, too, he should be capable of developing an understanding of the nature of man as a social and political being. And he should be capable of mastering the arts that are involved in human relationships. Both are prerequisites of a successful management experience.

Possibly some of you are wondering when I will get to the subject of developing managerial skills. Frankly, I am not so much interested in the development of skills in the formal educational sense as I am in the development of a broader perspective on man, man's nature, and man as a member of society. Now, it is true that skills and attitudes will certainly need to be developed and we, in the educational world, must direct our attention to doing that. But I assume one other factor that I have not yet mentioned. It is that formal education will be only the *beginning* of the entire process, not by any means the *end* of it.

I would imagine that the young man of 22 to 24 will have perhaps completed a reasonable period of formal education which will, at that stage, simply enable him to move into an organization on a basis whereby he can initiate his contributions first to the organization and then to society as a whole. But, from that point on, there will be available to him full opportunity for a continuation of the learning experience—if not along the lines of this Learning Center, then in terms of individual company programs.

So far as the formal education process itself is concerned, there is something else we need to recognize. Those of us who are directly involved in the educational world are sometimes placed in the position of being expected to achieve results beyond our capabilities for fulfillment.

I see the formal educative process in our schools and our colleges as providing an environment in which learning of a certain sort can take place. But it will be incomplete unless we have a strong inter-action with other elements of the society that enable the maturing young individual to have experience beyond that of the classroom, beyond the experience of his fellows of the same age group. This in-teraction has been missing in the past. To me, this has been one of the limiting factors in our total educative structure—a situation which I would hope could be changed as we look to the year 2000.

What do I mean specifically? Simply that the young people of today have, in my judgment, been so much denied the opportunity of a real live experience in the world that surrounds them—and in which they're going to find their life and being—that it is no wonder they have developed attitudes that are sometimes regarded as hostile to business and its environment.

I ask you: Can we find means by which a larger proportion of our young people—particularly those whom we're going to think of as the eventual managers of our large corporations—can experience actual working relationships in a meaningful setting outside the classroom? Is this possible within *your* businesses?

Unless we can begin to move toward a system in which a part of the individual educative process takes place in our society as a whole—whether it be in the corporation or in government—we will simply be attempting in an artificial way to realize our educational objectives.

I'm also concerned that we utilize other resources in this educa-tive process during the first 21 to 24 years of a young person's life. School and college can do only a portion of the total job; if they seek to do more, I fear they will fail. And it isn't only the role of the cor-poration that's important in providing rich, live opportunities for learning.

I think fervently about the role of the church and about the role of the family. These are two great institutions in our society that, regrettably, have had a diminishing influence on the education of our young people. These two big areas must receive continuing at-tention if we are to re-establish a moral foundation for the attitudes and outlook of our future managers. A system without such a foun-dation in the end produces a society that lacks a *qualitative* aspect.

So I would call for an educational program that goes considerably beyond the formal organization of elementary and secondary school, college, and university. I hope for a much broader involvement of individual in society during his formative years.

Listen for a moment to the students who are meeting in Baltimore this week. (I do not speak on behalf of the National Students Association, but I recognize the validity of some of their grievances.) They have been telling us for some time, "You're too paternalistic. We are young people of ability. We want the kinds of learning experience that will be meaningful in terms of our maturation and development as human beings."

All too often we shut them off, denying them the opportunity to participate in the very processes we would like to have them learn something about if they are to be the managers of the future.

They ask, "How can we possibly develop experiences that will give us self-reliance and the ability to manage our own affairs unless you give us the opportunity to do so?" This, increasingly, is the cry of the young person on the campus. This is essentially the underlying thesis of the group that's meeting in Baltimore. As adults we shy away and complain, "They're trying to take over."

But I don't think they really are. Some of them would like to take over, but they learn better quickly enough when they are given the chance.

I'm glad to say that at Tulane we constantly and consciously try to provide opportunities in which the student's capabilities will be tested. Students have an increasing degree of responsibility for the management of their affairs.

Of course, if we are to have managers in the future, their learning experiences must start, I suggest, much earlier than at graduation from college. I propose that we move toward an educational pattern that has built into it opportunity to succeed or fail. Indeed, some failures along the way and a recognition of the requirements of adjustment to meet the problems that failure produces may be most important to a future manager. Let us be tolerant when young people stumble or fumble, recognizing that they are in a learning setting and that they can't be perfect the first time around. Frankly, I don't see perfection in the adult world and I wonder why it is expected in our youth.

Thus, for the manager in the year 2000, I anticipate a broad extension of the training function to places of employment during the first few years after college.

The development of the neophyte manager will certainly encompass a complex accumulation of skills. In fact, here is where I think the skills aspect of preparation will come much more forcibly into the picture. After the completion of the basic educational program—which, from my point of view, should be heavily oriented toward an understanding of man, his nature, our society, and its interaction with other societies throughout the world—the first years of a person's employment might well be a vital and dynamic challenge as the new graduate confronts the business corporation, a government agency, or other employer. He must, in short, develop the wisdom that grows out of the achievement of goals essential to the well-being of the organization with which he is associated.

There can be, then, no relaxation of our persistent attention to strengthening and improving key people for successive levels of managerial responsibility. And, to repeat, we should start that process just as early in the educational setting as possible.

The implications of all this for the world of education are obvious. Certainly a continuous program of both formal and informal experiences is called for. I see the Manager Learning Center as making a definite contribution to this process of continuing education.

I suspect, Larry Appley, that you will, as you have in the past, be able to teach those of us who are engaged in the formal educative process some very good tricks about how to get the job done. We appreciate having the opportunity to feast at your table. It's been a great experience to see how you take the young neophyte and transform him into a functioning responsible individual.

Several years ago, Vannevar Bush, who then was Merck's chairman of the board, talked about management as a profession. (He had been writing on that subject, as some of you may recall, for a long time.) He talked about the ministry of the professional and individual human needs—a characteristic theme of those who speak about any profession. I was impressed in 1960 when Van made that address, and I was impressed again upon rereading it in preparation for these few remarks. Among other things, he said this: "It is by no means fully recognized that the profession of management exists."

For those who believe in our system and who would perpetuate it, there can be no more rewarding effort than to see that this recognition becomes general and real.

I do propose the dissemination of propaganda. I mean, in essence, that the professional attitude should be enhanced and emphasized whenever men of business gather.

I mean especially that the neophytes entering the long ladder which leads to great responsibility should become inculcated early with a professional spirit.

And, above all, I mean that there should be an increasing solidarity among members of the profession—not just in formal ways but in terms of those subtle influences which are exceedingly powerful in the growth of mutual understanding. I suggest a willingness to talk frankly combined with an exclusiveness. I would make it clear that true membership in a professional group of managers is highly desirable and can be obtained only by living the life of a professional man and securing the accolade of one's fellows.

Management as a profession still has a long way to go. It certainly is not going to be defined solely by the schools of business administration. In my judgment, the managers of the future will come from a much broader cross section of the total educational community than just the schools of business administration (even our distinguished graduate schools).

I suggest that one of the trends we will see in this last third of the century will be the further emergence of the concept of management as a profession. And this in itself will have an important bearing upon the nature of the educational preparation which the schools and colleges will be called upon to undertake.

We've all seen the great swings that have occurred and the great pressures that have been exerted on educational institutions as they have attempted to respond to the need to prepare young people for a profession. We can look at any of the older professions and begin to understand what happens when particularly strong individuals and groups achieve a dominant position and insist on the educational schemes they feel are the important ones.

Professional education has been confounded by such prophets. Examine the history of medical education, of legal education, or of education for dentistry or pharmacy. It's a simple matter to identify the strong movements which for a period of time dominated the scene in any one of the professions.

What I'm suggesting is this: As we attempt to define and promote management as a profession, we need to be alert to the possibility that the strong, dominant individuals in the professions may, by their very nature, either preclude educational changes or establish their own skill- and technique-orientation.

We are approaching the time when management as a profession will surely have greater recognition. When that day arrives, I hope, we educators will be in a position to respond with training that will be meaningful and constructive, and that will help us to prepare managers for the year 2000 and beyond. These managers will have the sense of responsibility and dedication to the dignity of work, to the ordered society, and to the qualitative aspects of life which, in the end, must be the significant influences that are brought to bear.

MR. BICKMORE: Thank you very much, Dr. Longenecker, for your lucid explanation of the position of education for the manager in the year 2000. I'm sure that we can take comfort in your remarks that the field of education will rise to the challenge and do its part to prepare the manager for the important role he will have in the year 2000.

I was interested in the statement you made at the beginning of your speech that we must get on with the job. It reminded me of a passage in the Bible, I think, which says, "With all of thy getting, get understanding." Then somebody paraphrased this a little bit and said, "With all of thy getting, get going." And I think that's what you're telling us—that we can't be late; we must prepare, we must be moving ahead.

Today, as we take a look at this entire problem, we're faced with the situation that undoubtedly by the year 2000 the population will be so great, the peoples involved will be so many, the businesses will be so large, and the government will be playing such an important role that there will not be any place for them to fight one another. The decisions will just be too great.

In a little corner store, two or three or four members of the family can have different ideas about how the business should be run and it won't be too disastrous. But if, in a big corporation, people have equal voices but different feelings and ideas, then we do have a definite problem. And so it is with world problems today. They're building up to the point where, unless we have a consensus of the large important groups—government, labor, the business community, and people in general—we will be in a bad way.

I liked your admonition that we should be having a broader outlook on education for management than is implied in the mere acquiring of skills, and that the time devoted to getting an education will be much greater in the future than it has been in the past. I think this is what Frank was telling us when he said that the number of man-years people spend in the labor force will be much fewer than ever before because they will spend more time being educated to begin with. And not only will they delay entering the job market but, because the age for compulsory retirement is getting lower and lower they will move out of it earlier. Moreover, people in management, even after they reach top company levels, will be going back to school continually to update their knowledge and skills. So we can see the importance of education and the role it is going to play.

I couldn't help but notice, also, that you were talking about education and not schooling. There's a big difference between the two. Some people go to school all their lives and never become educated; other people don't get much formal schooling and become quite highly educated. I suspect Abraham Lincoln was probably the most outstanding example of the latter type.

Also, Dr. Longenecker, I want to underscore your remarks with respect to the role of the family and the church. We all know how important they are in this whole process of education—not schooling—and in preparing the manager for the year 2000.

Now I'm wondering whether it would be in order, Frank, to permit one question to be asked each of these people. Do we have enough time? Would you like to come up, Dr. Walton, and be the first to respond?

VOICE FROM AUDIENCE: I'd like to ask all four the same question. If any of them alluded to it, I didn't hear the answer, although it may have been implied in what they said. At any rate, taking what I heard in the narrowest sense, we're assuming that in the year 2000 we're still going to be this same little island between the Pacific and Atlantic and between Mexico and Canada. Yet I'm sure it's on all our minds that the businesses for which we're going to educate and train managers will be truly global enterprises. I ask the educators: What

are you doing in your curriculum right now to teach a boy accounting and qualify him to become a CPA? Do you tell him that Italians
keep four sets of books? That's one of the many things he has to
know if he's going to work for Don Mitchell, because in the kind
of companies Don buys and operates the accountant is going to have
to convert those four sets into one.

Again, when you teach the social sciences, do you show how we
Americans can relate to the great majority of people outside the
United States who don't really want to be like us—who want to stay
the way they are yet have to co-occupy this world with us?

In teaching government, when you speak so magnificently of the
small changes which suddenly are having enormous effects, do you
point out that 20 or 30 years ago, U.S. fiscal policy could be adjusted
simply in the context of what happened in the United States and we
didn't have to worry about the balance of payments—whereas now
we can't change our interest rates because, if we did, there would be
an immediate reaction in world financial circles?

I didn't mean to make a speech. I'll stop. But I will ask each of you:
How do you see this world in the year 2000? And how do you see the
role of this magnificent Learning Center in preparing us for the fact
that the world's people are getting very, very close together—either
dangerously or gloriously?

MR. BICKMORE: Shall we start with you, Dr. Walton?

DR. WALTON: There are three prongs to this question. I'm going to
ignore the last because I think the Comptroller General could more
appropriately answer it. Let me take the first two that our friend has
identified. First, he mentioned the emergence of the multinational
or international corporation and asked what we are doing about it.
Second, he mentioned certain areas of managerial training, notably
accounting, in which the techniques learned may not be suited to the
culture or the values of the people to whom the techniques may be
applied. What, he asks, are we doing to remedy matters?

In answer to the first half of the question, it is true that we don't
stress sufficiently to our students the fact that one of the most interesting visions of our founding fathers was what amounted to an early
concept of a common market. By a stroke of genius we built into our
system provision for accepting a new state as an equal, once it

reached a certain degree of maturity. But, having done that, we were a little bit slow in seeing that with our deep concern for states' rights and local interests—the Jeffersonian legacy—the corporation by definition was going to create a national society and that it would respond to a national common market. That's a rather inadequate preliminary to the notion that the corporation is going to have a tremendously significant role to play in international business. This is true even in societies that are more tightly centralized than our own, largely because it's such an effective instrument for harnessing human resources within a voluntary constraint pattern.

Five or eight years ago I doubt that there were five business schools that actually had programs in international business. We have them today. I don't think that progress has been nearly as satisfying as some of us might have hoped, possibly because we've brought into the scholarly team people who are traditionally international economists but don't understand the full range of cultural values. I do believe, however, that in a world whose shrinkage is making us all part of one community, that the exchange experience—you know, a year in Paris or Rome—will be as common among youngsters as a chance to work a summer in the local A&P store when I grew up. I think our theoretical refinements will be much sharper in the next decade than they have been in the past, and I see that the effort has in fact been started.

As to the second half of the gentleman's question, I'm glad he used accounting techniques as an illustration. Accounting is, in many respects, the language of business. It's quantitative and precise, but beyond the precision and quantification are certain enormous assumptions. I am delighted to see that these are coming into the literature, along with the standard books on profit and loss, double-entry bookkeeping, and the like, more and more books concerned with accounting's social role. (The typical Latin American accountant, I understand from my reading, feels himself totally the servant of his client; he has no concern for society as a whole.) So these things are slowly beginning to change—and I would suspect that the rate of change, and therefore our regard for the international dimension, will increase rapidly.

Whether we can absorb this change fast enough, and whether we have, as Herb said, the wisdom to use it well, I'm not sure. All I can say is that, when we talk about university systems or formal education, it's well to remember that the scholar begins with a question and, normally, he asks only the questions that his discipline can answer. The human condition, however, requires an interdisciplinary approach, and it's going to take a little bit of innovation in higher education before we get the kind of response I think we need.

MR. STAATS: One graphic way to indicate the government's role in this changing world dimension is that prior to World War II we had only one agency with personnel stationed abroad. We have something like 14 agencies today. Also, one of the reasons for our present high standard of living in this country today is our heavy reliance upon foreign investments and the utilization of foreign raw materials—this is a truism that is not sufficiently recognized. In general, our relations with other peoples are becoming more and more a sensitive area, and government will have to play a part in solving the problems involved, not so much in diplomatic as in commercial terms. The Department of Commerce, the Department of Agriculture, the Atomic Energy Commission, and many others are fully aware of this. Our recent difficulties with Canada, I think, serve to dramatize just how delicate the problems can be in light of U.S. investments there and our reliance on Canadian sources of raw materials.

Then, of course, there is another aspect of this growing interest on the part of government in providing a stimulus to educating in foreign languages, not only because of the closer cultural ties that are beginning to prevail today but also because of the need for scientific and other personnel to share information.

DR. LONGENECKER: We are constantly perplexed with respect to the development in the college and university world of competencies that the business world has already developed so well in its international operations. Corporations that have functioned on a multinational basis have gained experience that is not yet, by any means, fully available to college and university instructors. We recognize this and are trying to do something about it.

In December of this year the deans of business schools and some of their faculty members will meet at Tulane University to examine how the formal educative process should be adapted to enrich the experience of students who will eventually serve you in industry. In this effort, there is a most important role for the world of business and industry itself to play.

I'm constantly impressed by the way one U.S. corporation handles its international affairs. It is remarkable to see the quality of leadership developed over a period of nearly 40 years in overseas operations and the knowledge its personnel have acquired of political and social trends in many countries throughout the world. This is the expertise that ought to be brought back, summarized, and made available to the present generation of students if they are to live and work effectively in a complex world.

Certainly, the question of the European Common Market that was skirted a moment ago is of enormous significance. Do we really understand what is happening in Europe today in terms of the changes that the Common Market represents? Are we actually prepared to instruct our students with respect to the influence of the recent trade negotiations leading to the elimination of trade barriers? Will it really be a free-trade world in which we operate our international divisions and subsidiaries?

Somehow we need to develop an alertness to these important questions and forceful movements of change occurring beyond our continental shelf. We are at a stage in this development that indicates some promise for the future, but not by any means the kind of promise I would like to hold forth. Yet, when you realize that the educational system of the United States has long had a serious deficit in the international area, and that for the past 15 years or so we've been trying to develop competence in it, you surely must admit that we've made some progress.

This progress is not yet adequate to deal with the kind of engagement American businessmen will have with their counterparts throughout the world in the very near future. We need to address ourselves increasingly to this question you've raised. As we try to attain competence, we need your help.

MR. NUNLIST: Worthington Corporation happens to be a company that manufactures in 14 nations and sells in 95. We have 5,000 employees overseas, and only 15 of them are Americans.

About a year ago I was at a conference with 30 Latin American businessmen and about 10 North Americans. We got into quite a heated discussion about why Latin Americans demanded majority ownership in corporations. The argument proceeded along this vein: Why do you demand majority ownership when after all, we furnish the capital, we furnish the know-how, and we furnish the personnel? Till, finally, a charming Panamanian stood up and said, "Yes, you have the know-how, but we have the know-who."

Realistically speaking, though, we do tend to make false assumptions about this sort of thing. As Americans we're a very proud people—in fact, we're vain about our business abilities, and we sometimes overlook the fact that there are tremendous business abilities abroad. England functioned successfully in international commerce before we even became a nation, and the English have educated their people to think internationally.

It's an interesting concept, Elmer, to note that, under the Mexican Government's budget for next year, 30 percent will be spent for education—higher education—and 10 percent for defense. And it isn't just Mexico. The nations of the world, whether they are industrially sophisticated or whether they are just emerging into the industrial era, are conscious of the fact that they have to develop know-how as well as know-who, and they're doing it very rapidly.

I suggest that maybe America is in fact a Johnny-come-lately to international business. Perhaps it isn't our job to educate the rest of the world in how to do business; maybe the rest of the world can educate us. I'm not at all sure whether a multinational corporation, as Clarence described it, is really an American corporation with a lot of international subsidiaries or whether it's not a sort of United Nations in which business plays a very important role.

We at Worthington have decided that political boundaries and economic boundaries are not the same thing. We do not analyze the business that we do in France or in North Africa. We analyze the business that we do in the various trading areas of the world—for instance, the interesting little common market developed by Iran and Pakistan and Turkey. Our statistics tell us, not how much business we do in one country, but how much business we do in a given trading area.

I think we sometimes tend to overburden ourselves with worries about political problems that may have an impact on business when, in fact, the state of our economy and the progress of this nation are such that perhaps we ought to be concerning ourselves more with the problems of social welfare. Let me illustrate. Elmer, I believe, stated that according to our 1967 federal budget we spent more than $100 per capita on research. Yet 52 of the 105 members of the United Nations have a GNP of less than $100 per capita, so that we, in this country, spent more for research than the total gross income of the average citizen of half the world. That's not going to last too long! Things *have* to change, and they are changing very, very rapidly.

It seems to me that we are at the point where we are beginning to import know-how from other nations of the world. And with this happening I say that in America—which is nothing more than a conglomerate of all kinds of different people (not only the melting pot but a stereo pattern of all the rest of the world) our vanity may be misplaced.

MR. BICKMORE: At this point I should like to thank our able team of speakers for their wonderful contributions. We have been very fortunate to be able to learn from them. We congratulate them on their presentations. And, at the same time, I would also like to thank all of you in the audience. You've been attentive, interested, and pleasant. It's been a wonderful morning.

Opening Remarks

DON G. MITCHELL
Chairman of the Board, General Time Corporation; and
Chairman of the Board, American Management Association

We come at last to the formal dedication of this Manager Learning Center building. I'd like to announce that any of you who have not yet had ample opportunity to go through the Center are welcome to inspect the facilities. The staff will be available this afternoon to guide anyone who may be interested.

Now I shall ask the Reverend Mr. Ross, of the First Baptist Church of Hamilton, to lead us in prayer.

Invocation

REVEREND VERNON H. ROSS
Minister, First Baptist Church, Hamilton, New York

Lord, our God, Thou who hast given us life and seen that it is good, Thou who hast given mankind dominion over all the works of Thy hands, Thou who hast ordained that man should fill the earth and subdue it, we turn to Thee most naturally at this moment of joyous dedication to express our thanksgiving to Thee for what has been brought into being here. We pray Thy blessing upon the work and purpose and program of this Research Center.

We see in this institution, our Father, a very significant part of Thy creative work for our world: the training of men and of women in the wise and efficient administration of the natural resources which Thou hast given to us for the good of all mankind. We pray, our Father, that this Research Center may become a power for peace and for goodwill in our time. We thank Thee, O Lord, for every challenge which demands the very best of us; and in particular, at this moment, we thank Thee for those men whose vision, imagination, courage, and hard work have brought this institution into being against heavy odds. We thank Thee, O Lord, for the gift of a mind and the desire to use it, for the gift of the heart and the capacity to love, for the gift of a soul and the continual opportunity to enlarge it.

To this end, our Father, we dedicate this institution and ourselves and pray always, our Father, that we may give Thee both honor and glory, now and forevermore. Amen.

MR. MITCHELL: Many predictions have been made during the course of this meeting. Arrangements have been made to gather the statements and the opinions that have been expressed here, and some of the information that reposes within these walls, and place them in a time capsule. Mr. Kastens will tell you about this.

Explanation of the Time Capsule

MERRITT L. KASTENS
Director, AFMR Manager Learning Center

Our colleagues in the field of psychology tell us that the mark of learning is change; that the only way you can measure learning is by change. Since we are dedicating a Learning Center here today, we are therefore introducing an instrument of change into the management community.

We've heard during the last two days some very knowledgeable predictions about what will be the nature of the changes in management practice during the remaining years of this century. Since this Learning Center has been built and is being operated under the auspices of a research foundation, it is appropriate that we take some steps to measure the nature of those changes.

As part of the Learning Center program, we have assembled here what is undoubtedly an unparalleled record of the practice of management in the United States at the present time. Well over 1,000 organizations have provided us with the intimate details of just how they carry out individual, specific management steps. Current technology permits us to condense this entire record into the two small canisters that some of you may have seen earlier in the Mitchell Memorial Library. These two small cylinders have been especially desiccated over a period of some weeks now and sealed by the Eastman Kodak people, who assure us that the records contained therein will survive indefinitely.

As soon as the transcript of these two days' discussions has been obtained, it too will be suitably prepared and placed in a larger canister made of a very new, very unusual alloy—not stainless steel—which was developed for use primarily in space vehicles. This record of our proceedings, plus the record of the current practice of management, will then be bathed in an inert atmosphere and the entire capsule welded shut to assure its integrity for the foreseeable future.

It is our intention to recover this capsule on August 22nd in the year 2000 and at that time to compare the nature of the management practices of the period with those of 1967. It will then be possible for us to indulge in the always interesting enterprise of second-guessing our speakers of the past two days.

We fully expect that things will have changed substantially. We know that in the past 33 years there have been fundamental changes in the practice of management. In retrospect, as good Monday-morning quarterbacks, we can look back to the research experiments and findings of the 1930's and 1940's and see the foreshadowing of the tremendous developments in management skill and knowledge which have marked this past third of a century.

We hope that we have been perceptive enough here to identify the current developments and trends which will determine the direction of the management evolution in the last third of the century. May I extend an invitation to all of you to join us on August 22nd in the year 2000.

MR. MITCHELL: In 1948, the American Management Association was 25 years old. It was a struggling organization with a few thousand members and a total income of some $450,000 annually. Its then president, Alvin Dodd, was rapidly approaching retirement age. He selected a committee of four from among his board of directors and gave them the job of selecting his successor. I was a member of that committee.

Alvin Dodd charged the committee with finding an able man who was willing to dedicate the rest of his life to raising professional management to the status and significance of the other learned professions. We found our man. He was at the time a top executive and board member of one of the great mail-order corporations of America. He proved the sincerity of his interest in our cause by accepting the presidency of AMA at a salary which was approximately one-third of the amount he was then receiving. He has proved his dedication to the cause by his tireless effort and his expert guidance of AMA, in the 19 years since then, to its present position as the largest of all professional associations—with an income from services rendered during this past year, affiliates included, of more than $22 million.

Today's dedication represents the culmination of one of this man's dreams. Over the years there have been many others. Here are some of them: In 1949, the starting of AMA seminars. In 1950, the first AMA program on the Pacific Coast. In 1951, the start of the AMA four-week Management Course. In 1955, the beginning of AMA programs here in Hamilton. In 1956, the founding of the International Management Association. In 1957, the establishment of the AMA Academy at Saranac. In 1960, The American Foundation for Management Research was founded, and it was followed in 1961 by The Presidents Association, headquartered here in Hamilton. The year 1962 saw our affiliation with the American Institute for Foreign Trade in Phoenix, Arizona, and in 1963 Operation Enterprise, our Hamilton youth program, got under way. And now, in 1967, we have this wonderful AFMR Manager Learning Center.

This is surely a record that from anyone's point of view should be sufficient for a full lifetime of work. But, in the considered judgment of this man, it is only the beginning. It is, therefore, with great personal pride that I introduce to you the man who, more than any other, is responsible for the prestige and respect in which professional management is held today throughout the world: my close personal friend and long-time colleague, Larry Appley.

MR. APPLEY: As I stand here at this moment, I just have to be the happiest man in the world. If there is anyone happier, I hope he'll step forward.

In the first place, I have received a heart-warming and deeply appreciated introduction from a friend and a business associate of 37 years. It is very meaningful to have Don introduce me as he has. In the second place, I'm extremely happy because of your reaction to the kind of program we've had here these past few days, and I'm particularly appreciative of those who have been part of that program. It has been a magnificent one which will have a tremendous impact for many years to come.

Furthermore, I'm extremely happy because it was 40 years ago, on the 1st of September, that I married a beautiful young lady by the name of Ruth Wilson in Ohio. Three days later we arrived in Hamilton, where I started my first full-time job as an instructor at Colgate University. This place means much to Ruth and me, and she shares with me at this time some of the words of appreciation that are being expressed.

Further contributing to this happiness, the president of Colgate University, Dr. Vincent M. Barnett, presented the keynote address of this dedication—and magnificent and challenging it was. My mind can't help but go back over these 40 years of constructive relationship with Colgate, a relationship that has contributed much to my life. For once I am extremely happy about an obligation. It is no coincidence that my new office is at the end of the wing of this new building looking down over the valley where I can see Colgate on the side of the hill. My associations with it have been that meaningful in my life.

I am extremely happy, too, about the unusually fine relationships I have enjoyed with a man by the name of Donald Burch, who put up this building without a contract. First we planned a hole in the ground; then we planned to put something in it, then something on it—and now you see what has happened. Step by step, we worked out the problems together, and we all take our hats off to Don Burch for this incredible job that has taken just a little more than ten months. During that time, I've had the privilege of meeting his workmen and his subcontractors, and a finer group of people I've never met on a job of this kind.

I also am extremely happy to be identified with organizations that have as fine people in them as do AMA and AFMR—splendid and magnificent people. Many literally worked day and night and weekends, some of them so hard that they became ill in the process. The dedication, loyalty, and performance that have been demonstrated here just cannot be exceeded.

It is a great source of happiness to me that there is present in this audience, as he has been throughout the program, Philo W. Parker, former chief executive of the Standard Vacuum Oil Company, who gave me my first opportunity to try to prove that professional management would really work in a business situation. And here is Dr. Eugene Bewkes, president emeritus of St. Lawrence University, who was an associate of mine on the faculty here years ago, then joined me at Vick Chemical, and later did a magnificent job as one of my associates during World War II in Washington. And we have in this audience Dr. Lillian Gilbreth, whom you've come to know and love if you did not know her before—one of the greatest pioneers in the science of management. Her personality and her work and teachings have meant much to me in my life. These are all people who have had a profound impact on the profession we're honoring today. Without them we would not be here.

More happiness arises from living among the splendid people of the Chenango Valley, in the village of Hamilton, on the shores of Lake Moraine. I've been around this world a bit, and people just don't come any finer.

And, finally, I'm extremely happy to stand on this spot in the presence of Mrs. Lewellyn Lamb. Mr. Lamb, Sr., was here for the laying of the cornerstone in the midst of this property that belonged to him, and the Lamb homestead is right in front of us across the road behind the beautiful maples. The Lambs are one of the finest families ever raised in any community. Mr. Lamb made property available to us as we needed it for our airport and other facilities of the Association. I want to pay him tribute, and I want to pay tribute to Mrs. Lamb.

So now maybe you'll permit me to say I'm the happiest man in this world as of this moment.

Dedication Address

LAWRENCE A. APPLEY
President, American Management Association, Inc. and
The American Foundation for Management Research

The evolution of management as a profession is, in my humble opinion, the most dramatic development in any segment of our society during the past quarter of a century. Management as a profession began to take shape in the late 1800's. It received some impetus in World War I. The most tangible recognition of it as one of the great professions of the world came during World War II. It was then that management was put to its greatest test in history, and it was proved that he who can manage can manage anything.

The fantastic transition from a wartime to a peacetime economy following World War II, without economic or human disaster, created a rapidly increasing demand for managers that was wholly unanticipated. With this came a demand for formal management development such as no one had predicted. Two facts bore in upon those who were extremely reticent to accept them: that one did not have to be experienced in a business to be able to manage it and that managers can be made as well as born.

The history of the American Management Association is evidence of these observations. AMA is an educational institution—dedicated to education in management, for management, and by management. It was founded by pioneers who believed in management as a profession and who believed that one could be trained for it. In 1948, AMA celebrated its 25th year. Its income was $434,000 that year, and fewer than 6,000 managers attended its conferences. On June 30, 1967, AMA completed its 44th year. Its income was very close to $19 million, and more than 100,000 executives participated in its functions. In the next five years it will more than double in income and in participants.

While this has been going on in the American Management Association, the same kind of development has been taking place in our universities and colleges, in other professional societies, with management consultants, and within companies through their intracompany training activities.

A reason for confidence in the observation that the impact of this development is the greatest of any in the past quarter of a century is the importance of management to human endeavor. Professional management makes the future; it does not wait for it. Professional management attains predetermined objectives by organizing and guiding physical and human resources toward that end. Up until World War II, management flew pretty much by "the seat of its pants." It was a leave-it-to-chance atmosphere. One took things as they came without any realization of one's power to change these things and to alter their course.

One might argue that technology has experienced a more dramatic development than any other segment of our society. Technological discovery, however, could not have been utilized to the extent it has been without the increasing capability of management to make it useful. Depressions and world wars have been prevented over the past quarter of a century through the increasing competency of leadership.

It is with modesty that the American Management Association bows in accepting recognition for the part it has played in the development of professional management as a concept and as a practice. Managers representing practically all segments of our society—theologians, educators, government administrators, labor leaders, journalists, agriculturists, and business executives—have sat at its conference tables and benefited thereby. This has taken place not only at home in the United States, but also abroad in a most significant manner.

In the performance of its work, the American Management Association follows a very definite process:

1. Through its meeting program, its research, and its publications, it aids tremendously in the development of a very specific, precise, clear, simple, and orderly concept of what professional management is and how it operates. (If we can influence how and what a person thinks, we can influence what he does.)
2. It aids in the development of a common vocabulary among professional managers, and particularly among the managers of single organization units, thereby aiding communication and understanding within the profession.
3. It generates and revitalizes an enthusiasm which inspires continuing effort on the part of managers to improve their professional capabilities.
4. It assists those with such enthusiasm in activating successful professional management practices within their own institutions.

Over the past several years AMA has reached a level of professional competence, of world prestige, and of financial stability that has enabled it to take a profoundly significant and extremely essential step in the fulfillment of its growing responsibilities. I refer to the founding and functioning of The American Foundation for

Management Research. While the Foundation is independent of the American Management Association it was founded by, its work is increasingly essential to the future of AMA, as well as to management as a profession.

It became obvious that the most serious problem with important research findings is putting them to use—or, in other words, the activation of such findings; the fourth category mentioned above. In order to aid in increasing the effective utilization of continually unfolding management know-how, The American Foundation for Management Research has inaugurated the AFMR Manager Learning Center in Hamilton, New York. The Center has been pilot-tested during the past year at the White House on the hill to the north.

The very heart of the AFMR Manager Learning Center is the Donald W. Mitchell Memorial Library. This was the beginning of this great institution which we are now dedicating. Donald W. Mitchell was a very successful young executive with the Corn Products Company in Chicago, Illinois. He was an avid student of management literature. On numerous occasions, he would visit our library in New York and would consult with me personally at some length as to the best sources of information to pursue in his search for greater management capability.

"Mitch" Mitchell's last days were fraught with discomfort, but his one great request was for us to continue to send books and periodicals to his bedside. This was very carefully done. A graduate of Duke University with a law degree, the father of four beautiful children, Mitch was taken from us by Him who knows more than all mankind as to why.

Young Donald was the son of Constance W. and Don G. Mitchell. Don Sr. has for many, many years been active in the affairs of the American Management Association. He joined AMA at the same time I did in 1930; and if I have no other indebtedness to this institution, that which I owe for the friendship that has ensued over these years is great enough.

Don Sr. is the chairman of our Board of Directors and chairman of our Exeuctive Committee. He is constantly participating in our activities, and his wife, Connie, accompanies him as he travels to many points throughout this world in the service of professional management. We are indebted to these fine people for providing what was necessary to start the Library from whence has come this Learning Center.

The Manager Learning Center contributes a very specific type of help to those executives in any walk of life who would like to make their work as managers more effective.

1. The Learning Center *provides a discipline.* By making an engagement with the Center, one finds it easier to do what he knows he should do than it would be if it were left to his own self-discipline. When a date has been made to visit the Center and to utilize its staff and facilities, executives will keep that date.

2. The activation of the practices of professional management is a *habit-forming process.* Habit forming requires coaching and close supervision for a period of time until new habits have replaced old ones. The Manager Learning Center experience provides exactly that.

3. Better management requires *more and better information made quickly available.* In the Learning Center, an individual executive or a management team can learn more about management or some basic phase of it in one week than he or they could previously learn in one year. Furthermore, that information will be kept updated. The very latest and finest information retrieval systems will be maintained in the Center at all times, emanating from the Donald W. Mitchell Memorial Library.

4. *Instruction is paramount.* When any leader, any manager, is too big to learn any more, his time has come to step aside and let younger and more responsive minds take over. The learning experience is a magnificent one—it is a continuing growth process. It is the intention of the AFMR Manager Learning Center to have specialists on its staff who are in a position to offer the very finest instruction possible.

The purpose of the AFMR Manager Learning Center, therefore, is to provide a discipline within which new habits will be formed, greater information acquired, and instruction and coaching provided, in such a way that the effectiveness of the individual, or the institution involved, cannot help but be increased.

The Center is dedicated to better management in every phase of organized society. It is not restricted to business management. A $65,000 grant has been awarded to Colgate University for an experiment in long-range planning for an educational institution. An offer has been made to Cazenovia College, and accepted by that institution, for the Center to underwrite the cost of a study in measuring teacher effectiveness. This community of Hamilton, New York, has expressed interest in having a study made of the hospital needs of this area so that its Community Memorial Hospital may have a greater chance of meeting future needs than it now has in terms of current requirements.

The officials of one of our great cities will be visiting us before the summer is out. The public school system of another metropolitan area has been inspired by its contact with us. The message is quite clear.

American business and industrial management made its mistakes, took its bloodbath, retreated within its shell, and learned its lessons well during the 1930's. World War II presented a great challenge, and it was met well. Joseph Stalin, standing up to his knees in the rubble of Stalingrad, stated that the greatest contribution to final victory was the fantastic miracle of American war production.

Since that time, the challenges have continued to present themselves: postwar transition to peacetime production; the Korean conflict on top of a booming U.S. civilian economy; the threat of depressions in 1958, 1962, and 1967; the unprecedented technological explosion; the increasing shortages of competent management talent.

Out of all of this, business and industrial leadership has recognized, formalized, and pursued management as a profession. It had to! It was back in the early 1960's that Dean Courtney Brown of the Columbia School of Business Administration said, "Management has now taken its place alongside of theology, education, medicine, law, and engineering as one of the great professions of the world."

Leadership in other segments of our society than business and industry has lagged behind. The message of industrial and business management is now coming through loudly and clearly. Religion, education, government, labor, and others are learning that the future can be made and that we do not have to wait for it. They are learning from the lessons of industrial and business management that uncertainty as to the future can be reduced. They are learning that it is ridiculous to sit back and let things happen when professional management would have prevented them from happening.

When we talk about professional management, we are talking about competent attainment of predetermined objectives as compared with letting things happen as they may. For example:

- In the *Reader's Digest* for August 1967, former President Dwight D. Eisenhower said: "The nation seems to be plunging to an era of lawlessness which, in the end, can lead only to anarchy. . . . We ought to be ashamed."
- Syracuse *Post-Standard* reporter Erwin Knoll wrote on July 25, 1967: "Only a makeshift apparatus exists within the Federal Government for dealing with the riots, and it serves mainly as a clearing house for information rather than as a center for action."

Professional management is action-oriented. If government is to be effective in meeting its increasing responsibilities in a rapidly changing society, then it had better take a lesson from industrial and business management and learn the significance of professional management and adopt its practices. I am not suggesting that government adopt business practices. I am suggesting that government and other major segments of our society adopt *professional management practices* as business is accepting them.

It is incredible that this nation can be crippled and the lives of its people endangered by strikes. The right to strike was introduced as a tool to equalize weak labor against strong management. It is outmoded, and dynamic professional management would introduce an effective substitute for it.

There is no rhyme nor reason to continuing inflation. Its continuation is evidence of the lack of the professional management concept in government. Anyone with an ounce of intelligence knows that when basic costs go up, prices have to go up; and when prices go up, you decrease the value of the dollar. Political pressures and professional management do not mix. One cannot ignore the causes for inflation for political reasons and expect to prevent it. It can, however, *be* prevented.

Think of a peace-dominated, democratic world sitting back and watching a belligerent nation build a wall right through the middle of a modern city and then sitting back while people get shot to death trying to get over, through, or under it! It is incredible! Think of a little island off the southeastern tip of the United States being permitted to become a burr under the skin of a great nation. It is hard to conceive. Think of a bragging, bullying, deceitful China causing the expenditures of lives and money which are now occurring in Vietnam. It is beyond the comprehension of most reasonable people.

These things did not have to happen. They can be prevented from happening. The more professional management there is in government, in the church, in education, the more the future can be what we would like it to be. It is our hope that we may be of some service toward that end.

It is with no ordinary gratification, it is with no mere satisfaction, it is with no small amount of pride that we now dedicate the Donald W. Mitchell Memorial Library and the Manager Learning Center to which The American Foundation for Management Research has given birth. May more and more people in positions of leadership and influence come to realize that in this quiet Chenango Valley, to and from which so many influential people have come and gone, lies a message of great importance to the world. Here is an institution dedicated as of this moment to

The advancement of human welfare
through
greater utilization of management knowledge.

MR. APPLEY: A salute from our fleet! [The two AMA jets fly overhead at this point.] Ladies and gentlemen, would you mind standing and facing the building? Dr. Gilbreth and Mrs. Appley will pull the veil from the plaque.

May I now repeat: Here is an institution dedicated to the advancement of human welfare through greater utilization of management knowledge. Will you now face the front once more? Mr. Mitchell, I will return the dedication service to you.

MR. MITCHELL: I am glad that I have had this opportunity to share with Larry Appley the great satisfaction of seeing the completion of this Management Learning Center which is so significant a part of his overall plan. I am glad, too, that I have had the opportunity of sharing with our distinguished speakers and panelists the knowledge and concepts which they have presented here. If I may be permitted to paraphase Abraham Lincoln, "I believe the world *will* note and long remember what has been said here—and will be a better place for what will be done here."

And now may I ask the Reverend Matthew J. Doran of St. Mary's Roman Catholic Church to conclude this meeting.

Benediction

REVEREND MATTHEW J. DORAN
Pastor, St. Mary's Roman Catholic Church, Hamilton,
New York

Almighty God, in Thy goodness Thou hast given man dominion over the things of this world. Desire is an imitation of Thy love. Take, we beseech Thee, these facilities that we may use our talents and abilities to think, plan, and accomplish for the welfare of all mankind. Direct, we beseech Thee, all our actions by Thy holy inspiration, to carry on this work by Thy gracious assistance, that every thought and action of ours may always begin from Thee and truly be happily ended through Christ our Lord. Amen.